T0316793

CANADIAN-AMERICAN PLANNING

The Seventh Annual Seminar of Canadian-American relations held at the University of Windsor brought together a number of distinguished participants, representing such interested groups as labour, business, and research, to discuss planning. The result is this volume which brings together some of the contributors to discussion of this important and controversial area of Canadian-American relations.

The noted economist HARRY G. JOHNSON begins by defining planning in the Canadian-American context. He then identifies several promising areas for joint planning. Subsequent papers on official and business planning echo the approach outlined in Dr. Johnson's definition, and stress the need for vision based on discernment of where we are and where we are going. These discussions are grouped into the categories Business, Labour, New Areas of Co-operation, Automation, and Technical Change.

Finally, PAUL YLVISAKER, Director of the Public Affairs Program for the Ford Foundation in New York, under the title "The Human Price of Planning" adds a cogent warning that this future focus, however skilfully it is related to present knowledge, may not be enough, pointing to recent events in the University of California at Berkeley and in Watts, California, as an indication of the importance of being prepared for and receptive to the immediate and unexpected. He suggests that planning for the cities of the future should be the most important concern for Canadian and American planners.

By bringing together a variety of viewpoints on some of the most relevant aspects of planning for the future this volume will provoke lively discussion, and provide a useful reference, for all those who will take part in planning for the future, and those who will be affected by it.

CANADIAN-AMERICAN PLANNING

The Seventh
Annual Conference on
Canadian-American
Relations, 1965

PUBLISHED FOR THE UNIVERSITY OF WINDSOR
BY UNIVERSITY OF TORONTO PRESS

CONTENTS

INTRODUCTION

THE WORD "PLANNING" conjures up in many people's minds the notion of rigid central direction of the affairs of a country, such as characterized the Russian economic system until a relatively few years ago, is practised by mainland China, and is frequently considered both necessary and desirable in the aspirant underdeveloped countries of the world. Others, drawing on observation of post-war developments in Europe and particularly in France, envisage a system of "indicative planning," in which the government, while not exercising rigid central control, lays down fairly specific targets for economic and social development and uses the wide variety of persuasive and coercive instruments at its command to enforce broad compliance with its specific objectives.

Planning in the first sense is quite alien to our North American traditions of political and economic freedom, and planning in the second sense, while far less abhorrent in many ways, is inconsistent with our traditional relationships between government and private industry. Both types of planning, however, are merely particular examples of approaches to planning, adapted to the special political and economic circumstances of the countries that employ them. In general, planning means attempting to foresee what alternatives the future may hold and to make the best of possible future developments, by whatever means are available in a particular social context. Planning in this sense is a necessary part of the activities of all individuals and of the societies or political entities within which they live. The difference between planning in the two systems just discussed, and planning in a free society of the Canadian-American type is that, in the latter, planning is largely effected by public discussion and voluntary co-operation and co-ordination of efforts by private individuals, enterprises, and governments.

Planning in this sense has become increasingly necessary and increasingly pervasive—in modern North America. One reason is the growing complexity of our economic and social organization. Another is the acceleration of social and economic change. A third is our increasing awareness, as a result of both experience and deliberate analysis and research, of the fact that changes in particular areas of our economic and social system may have far-reaching ramifications, the nature of which is by no means obvious either to those immediately involved in introducing change or to those affected by it. A fourth reason is the increasing political and economic interdependence among nations. All of these trends—essentially, towards increasing complexity and interdependence on the one hand, and towards increasing ability to analyse and predict developments on the other—have extended both the area of actual planning operations and the scope for wise and useful planning activities.

The trend towards broader and more far-ranging planning has been manifest in both Canada and the United States in recent years. In the area of planning for economic stability and growth, the trend has perhaps been more conspicuous in Canada, with the establishment of the Economic Council of Canada charged with responsibility for investigating and reporting on medium-term economic prospects and problems. But in the United States the Council of Economic Advisers, in its annual reports to the President under the Employment Act of 1946, has increasingly come to concern itself with medium- and long-term problems, such as economic growth, the effects of automation, the economic effects of discrimination against Negroes, and the causes of and cure for poverty. In designing their policies for stability and growth, moreover, both countries have more and more become aware of potentialities for conflict between them, arising from the strong interdependence created by their intimate trading relationships and the close integration of their capital markets, and the possibly disrupting effects on this relationship of interdependence of policies adopted from purely national considerations.

Planning for achieving economic stability and growth by the use of the fiscal and monetary powers of the central government, however, is only one element in the spectrum of planning activities. Other, and in some respects potentially more important, aspects are concerned with such problems as the development of natural resources, the exploitation of sources of energy, the conservation and development of water resources in the face of rapidly growing agricultural, industrial, and consumer demands for water, and the manifold consequences of the progressive urbanization and "metropolitanization" of our way of life. In many of these areas, the fact that Canada and the United States share the same continent and draw on the same pool of continental resources inevitably involves both the possibility of conflicts of interest and the potentiality of joint benefit from approaching the problems of planning on a continental rather than a national basis.

In past years, the annual seminar on Canadian-American Relations at the University of Windsor has concentrated on areas of actual or potential conflict in relations between the two countries. In discussing arrangements for the 1965 seminar, however, the Advisory Board decided that the time had come to shift to a more positive conception of Canadian-American relations; one that would emphasize the problems that the two countries have in common, problems from which they could learn from one another's experience, and problems whose solutions might be most fruitfully approached by co-operative investigation and action. It seemed to the Board that the time was right for a joint discussion and explanation of the area of planning, both because there has been little evaluation of the potentialities and limitations of the planning approaches that have been evolved in recent years, and because the topic of planning accorded ideally with the continuing purposes of the seminar. The program of the Seventh Annual Seminar was therefore designed around the central theme of planning, and the selection of speakers and topics aimed at illuminating the main areas of interest common to the two countries. It is hoped that the proceedings of the seminar, published in this volume, will be as interesting to the reader as they were to those who attended.

> The Advisory Board
> Canadian-American Relations Seminar
> University of Windsor

January 1966

CANADIAN-AMERICAN PLANNING

I. POSSIBILITIES AND LIMITATIONS OF JOINT PLANNING

HARRY G. JOHNSON*

THE TERM "PLANNING," in the context of Canadian-American relations, is something far removed from the central direction and control of economic activity by a political dictatorship which characterizes the economies of a number of countries in other parts of the world. It refers merely to the general process of attempting to take stock of the present situation and its evolving trends, predicting the general direction of future developments, assessing these in the light of generally accepted social and economic goals, and where necessary, formulating programs and policies designed to shape future developments as closely as possible to what is considered to be in the social interest. This general process is no more than the analogue, at the social level, of the responsible individual and the efficient business firm in our society which

*Professor of Economics, University of Chicago.

keep a careful eye to the future. Just as the main motivation for private planning is the prudent self-interest of the individual or business firm, so the main motivation of social planning is the prudent self-interest of these same entities in their capacity as members of society. And just as private planning can be carried on in thorough consistency with political democracy and a competitive economic system, so can social planning be carried on in thorough consistency with political democracy and economic freedom. In fact, one can go further, and maintain that some measure of economic and social planning is necessary if political democracy and economic freedom are to yield the full fruits of economic well-being and personal satisfaction and happiness to society's members. Planning in this sense is not exclusively, or even predominantly, the prerogative of government and its agencies; much relevant planning in our society is the work of voluntary and unofficial groups that have become concerned enough about some problem to gather and disseminate information and stimulate public discussion.

Social and economic planning in this sense has, on a broad interpretation, always been a feature of political life and government in Canada and the United States. Canadians are usually much more aware of this fact than are Americans, because in the early stages of their economic development Americans were more able than Canadians to rely on the natural forces of free competition to develop their portion of the North American continent. Planning in the United States was mostly concerned with the allocation of rights and opportunities for the application of private enterprise, whereas in Canada government action was necessary from the very beginning to supplement, reinforce, and improve on the efforts of private enterprise. This dissimilarity in historical necessity and experience survives to the present, both in a host of detailed differences with respect to which sectors and aspects of economic activity are considered appropriate or inappropriate subjects for governmental control or management, and in a general tendency for Canadians to be more pragmatic than Americans in their expression of preferences for private over public enterprise. Fundamentally, however, both countries have taken the pragmatic rather than the dogmatic view. While they have remained predominantly free-enterprise countries, enterprise has been constrained to exercise its freedom within a framework of democratic and voluntary planning.

While planning, in a very broad sense of the term, has always been characteristic of both countries, the need for conscious planning has been increasing rapidly over the past half century, as has the practice of planning in response to the need for it. Both trends are a consequence of the increasing complexity and interdependence of economic and social life, and specifically of the growth of scientific and technological knowledge, which has underlain the increase in economic efficiency that has made possible our high and rising standard of living. With the growing interdependence of economic life and private economic decisions, it has become increasingly necessary to take account of the aggregate consequences of private decisions, and to attempt to feed back to the decision-takers both information on these aggregate consequences, and guidance on the implications for each decision-taker of the decisions of others. With the growth of scientific knowledge—both of physical and biological phenomena and of how the economy and society function—it has become increasingly possible to forecast the consequences of current trends and to identify areas in which purely private decision-taking will produce undesirable consequences for which some kind of social remedial action or guidance is necessary. In short, both the need and the capacity for planning are a function of the growth of knowledge. More precisely, the need for planning arises from the fact that those who use new knowledge in the pursuit of private profit in a competitive economy rarely possess either the competence or the incentive to appreciate the full implications of such knowledge—and there is no reason to expect such omniscience of them—while at the same time the well-being of society as a whole increasingly depends on understanding these implications and taking steps to ensure that their total effect is in the social interest. Techniques for assessing these implications and calculating their results are readily becoming available.

The purpose of this paper is to explore the extent to which planning in both countries could be made more effective by co-operation between them, and the limitations to the possibilities of achieving more effective planning by joint action that may exist. In discussing the possibilities and limitations of joint planning I shall make substantial use of the report, *Canada and the United States: Principles for Partnership* (Ottawa: Queen's Printer, 1965), submitted by the Honourable Livingston T. Merchant and the Honourable A. D. P. Heeney. Prepared at the joint request of the Canadian Prime Minister and the President of the United States, the Merchant-Heeney *Report* considers the precepts and possibilities for co-operation between the two countries.

It is obvious at the outset that, for two sovereign nations that are involved in such a complex and pervasive relationship of interdependence as Canada and the United States, and yet differ so greatly in size and world importance, joint planning must be primarily a matter of consultation about joint or conflicting interests. The importance of consultation in the past, and the need for a strengthening and extension of already established techniques of consultation at all levels, are the main themes of the Merchant-Heeney *Report*. It lays particular emphasis on the need for consultation to begin at an early enough stage to be true planning, rather than the picking up of pieces in arrears, as consultation between the two countries has frequently been in recent years.

Considered as a technique of joint planning, consultation has two contrasting useful functions: the negative function of avoiding or minimizing conflicts and inconsistencies between the domestic planning activities and polices of the two countries, and the positive function of co-ordinating individual planning and action by the two countries, or initiating joint action for problems that transcend national boundaries and national responsibilities and powers.

The positive function of joint planning is the one that tends to capture the imagination. But, given the high degree of interdependence of the Canadian and American economies, the negative function may well be the more important, because the prosperity and growth associated with economic interdependence stem from a specialization and division of labour that depends on the maintenance of a stable framework of domestic and international economic policies, which could easily be disrupted by a change in economic policy on either side. The importance of the negative function tends to be underestimated, precisely because Canada and the United States have worked out fairly effective consultation machinery. A vast array of problems is disposed of quietly behind the scenes, without the general public being aware that an exercise in joint planning has been taking place. It is only when the consultation machinery breaks down—when it is ignored, or is brought to bear too late to be effective—that the importance of this function of joint planning becomes evident. Incidents of this kind have unfortunately been rather frequent in recent years; indeed, concern over their frequency was responsible for the commission of the Merchant-Heeney *Report*. The *Report* was based on a series of case studies of recent issues in Canadian-American relations, some of which were ultimately resolved satisfactorily and some not; and it may help to demonstrate the potential usefulness of the negative function of joint planning to describe these cases:

1. The introduction of a differentiated withholding tax, designed to induce "Canadianization" of the ownership and control of American subsidiaries in Canada, in the Canadian Budget of 1963; and the proposal by the United States administration in the summer of that year to introduce an interest equalization tax that took no account of Canada's special dependence on the United States capital market.

2. Canadian trade with Cuba.

3. Storage and possession by Canadian forces of nuclear weapons supplied by the United States.

4. The labour dispute in Great Lakes shipping and the legal position and rights of American unions in Canada.

5. The allocation of civil aviation rights.

6. Co-ordination of policies in the marketing of wheat.

7. The sharing of defence production.

8. The extraterritorial application of United States domestic legislation, specifically the United States Trading with the Enemy Act, anti-trust legislation, and Securities Exchange legislation.

9. Restrictions on the circulation of American magazines in Canada.

10. Control of oil and gas exports.

11. Fishing rights and the definition of territorial seas.

12. Working relationships between Canada and the United States in international organizations and contexts.

Many of these issues, as the *Report* notes, are of a type that is likely to recur; for they concern either matters of broad national policy or the regular conduct of economic affairs. There is therefore both the need and the opportunity for more effective consultation and joint planning to avoid or minimize conflict. On this subject the *Report*, from its examination of the cases listed, concludes (para. 35) that: "In every case that we have examined where difficulties have developed, and ultimately been satisfactorily resolved or accommodated, full and timely consultation has been an essential element in its disposition. Similarly, the absence of prior consultation, or the fact that such consultation as did take place was regarded as insufficient, has been a feature of many cases where an impasse has occurred and no acceptable compromise has been reached." This conclusion is the basis for the *Report's* many recommendations for the improvement of consultative machinery between the two countries. But the *Report* fully recognizes that the possibilities of resolving issues by consultation are limited, as are the possibilities of joint planning, by divergences of national interest and sentiment, and also by limitations of feasibility.

I turn now to the positive function of joint planning— the co-ordination of national planning, and the initiation of joint activities where the problems are international. For purposes of discussion, I find it convenient to distinguish between two broad spheres of potential joint planning, the sphere of relations between the two countries and the sphere of relations of the two countries with the outside world—the intracontinental and the extracontinental. These two spheres, however, overlap in some important problem areas, notably trade and international financial policy. I shall begin with the extracontinental sphere, both because it is the sphere I have studied more closely and because I believe that the needs and opportunities for joint planning in that sphere are both more pressing and less self-evident than in the intracontinental sphere.

The need for joint planning in the extracontinental

sphere is pressing, because the structure of the world economy and the balance of power in it have been changing rapidly, with the result that the existing institutional structure for regulating world trade and payments is no longer appropriate and requires substantial modification. The present institutional structure, consisting of the International Monetary Fund, the International Bank for Reconstruction and Development, and the General Agreement on Tariffs and Trade, was established some twenty years ago, as a result of an international planning effort in which Canada and the United States co-operated very closely. It largely embodied principles of international economic relations on which the two countries were in substantial agreement. The International Monetary Fund was intended to provide the combination of international liquidity and an internationally agreed adjustment mechanism (the ability to change exchange rates in cases of "fundamental disequilibrium") necessary to a smoothly functioning international monetary order. The General Agreement on Tariffs and Trade established principles for fair international trade, based on the principle of non-discrimination, and a mechanism for the multilateral liberalization of trade through the negotiation of tariff reductions on a reciprocal basis. The International Bank was designed to provide a steady flow of capital on easy terms to the less developed countries.

All three institutions, though they have performed usefully, have been displaced from the centre of the international picture by post-war events: the IMF has been overshadowed by the evolution of the dollar to the position of key international reserve currency; GATT has been subordinated to the domestic agricultural policy of the United States and its concern with the integration of continental Europe through the formation of the European Economic Community; and, the World Bank has been dwarfed as a source of development capital by the growth of bilateral development aid given for political, military, and humanitarian reasons. What is more important, is that strains have been developing within the areas of responsibility of the three institutions, and can only be resolved by substantial institutional and policy changes. In the area of international monetary organization, the prolonged period of United States deficits and European surpluses on the balance-of-payments account has led to mounting European resentment of the dominance of the dollar in world finance, to agreement that the international monetary system needs to be reformed, and to sharp disagreement over whether it should be reformed in an expansive internationalist way, by enlarging the IMF, or in a more restrictive nationalist way, by giving an international reserve role to the major European currencies. In the area of international trading relationships, the formation of the European Economic Community has brought the principles and practices of economic regionalism and discrimination into the centre of the GATT organization, with disruptive consequences which the United States has been unable to contain by the Trade Expansion Act. In the area of development finance, it has become apparent that the present volume of foreign aid is grossly inadequate for the prospective requirements of the developing countries; and for this and other reasons these countries have begun to press hard for trade preferences, commodity agreements, and other special arrangements designed to increase their export earnings.

In all three of these areas, the strains will have to be resolved by new institutional arrangements and policy changes, which will have to be worked out by the interplay of national interests and international consultation and negotiation. In all three areas, the interests of Canada and the United States are parallel enough to one another, and distinct enough from those of other nations or groups of nations, for there to be a basis for, and a joint advantage in, consultation and co-ordination of their approach to the problems. In the monetary field, Canada is now essentially a constituent of the dollar area, and has the same interest as the United States in reforming the international monetary system in a way that will permit the termination of present restrictions on access to the United States capital market. In the development field, both countries have a non-imperialistic interest in the less developed countries, both are averse in principle to the proliferation of discrimination and special treatment in international trading relationships, and both want to avoid disruption of their domestic markets by competition from low-wage producers in less developed countries.

It is in the field of international trade policy, however, that the need for co-ordination of approaches is most pressing; for the Trade Expansion Act will expire in less than two years time, and it is obvious that, whatever emerges from the Kennedy Round, the reluctance of the European Economic Community to respond to the American initiative for freer trade and the divergence of views between the two parties that has become apparent in the bargaining process will necessitate the formulation of a new commercial strategy by the United States. It will be recalled that the Canadian government of the time took no interest or part in the preparation of the Trade Expansion Bill. One consequence was that the Trade Expansion Act was far less favourable to Canada's trade-negotiating interests than it might have been, had Canada displayed any eagerness to co-operate with the United States in pursuing the act's objectives. Another consequence—or so at least one might conjecture—was that the primary negotiating authority of the act (the "dominant supplier" authority) was framed so as to depend on the validity of the United States administration's assumption that Britain would be admitted to membership in the European Economic Community. The rejection of Britain's application rendered that authority void of content and left the power to negotiate dependent on the far less attractive 50 per cent authority. Canadian participation in the planning of the approach to the Kennedy Round might have raised some doubt about the wisdom of assuming that Britain would be admitted to the EEC, and led to a less vulnerable specification of the negotiating authority. This is, of course, mere conjecture; but hindsight does suggest that a joint approach to preparation for the next round of GATT would substantially increase the likelihood of successful negotiation of further trade liberalization. What that approach should be, however, is a problem that requires much study and political calculation. One of the many ideas in the air is to strengthen the bargaining position of the United States and other non-EEC trading countries *vis-à-vis* the EEC by forming a free-trade area among the United States, Canada, and the United Kingdom or the European Free Trade Association countries as a group. Action along this line would obviously require joint planning of a high order. Such planning has already been initiated, on a private basis and in a conditional sense, by the studies of the problems and possible outlines of a free trade arrangement between Canada and the United States;[1] and the probable economic consequences of a Canadian-American free trade area are the subject of a major study by Paul and Ronald Wonnacott.[2]

Let us now turn from the extracontinental to the intracontinental sphere of potential joint planning. Here one

[1]Sperry Lea, *A Canada-United States Free Trade Arrangement: A Survey of Possible Characteristics* (Washington and Montreal, 1963).

[2]*A Possible Plan for a Canada-United States Free Trade Area* (Washington and Montreal, 1965).

can usefully distinguish between two aspects or facets of policy where joint planning could usefully be extended, aspects which can respectively be termed "management" policy and "framework" policy. The first term describes the policies employed to manage the over-all economy in pursuit of the objectives of high employment, price stability, economic growth, and balance in the balance of payments; these are frequently referred to as "stabilization policies." The second term describes those policies that set the framework of rules and relationships within which private competitive enterprise must operate; for present purposes, the most important of these are commercial policy, and other policies affecting the international mobility of goods, services, and factors of production.

For two countries so closely linked through trade and through capital flows as Canada and the United States, the general desirability of harmonizing and co-ordinating management policies is fairly self-evident; and in fact in the past such policies have been operated in substantial harmony in the two countries, though this has largely been the result of the policy-makers reacting independently in the same way to developments common to the two interlinked economies. The need for a more deliberate concerting of management policies has, however, become apparent as a consequence of new developments. In the first place, the return to a fixed exchange rate for the Canadian dollar, in 1962, meant that changes in Canada's international payments position or domestic economic policy, which previously would have resulted in changes in the exchange rate, would now result in changes in Canada's international reserves; and, given the concentration of Canadian trade and capital imports in the United States, such reserve changes would largely entail opposite changes in the United States balance of payments.

Secondly, the continuation of the United States deficit, and specifically the association of that deficit with private capital outflows from the United States, has led the administration increasingly to resort to intervention in foreign investment as a means of restraining the nation's deficit. Given the dependence of Canadian development on a substantial and sustained inflow of American capital, such interventions could be seriously disruptive to Canadian economic growth. In short, because of the close trade and investment relationship between the two countries, the adoption of policies, by either country, designed to improve its balance of payments is likely to have the main effect of worsening the balance of payments of the other. This is a troublesome situation because—contrary to what has frequently been asserted by Canadian officials in justification of a number of questionable recent policies—the basic disequilibrium in the international economy is not between Canada and the United States, but between the United States and the European countries. Its solution requires an improvement of the United States balance of payments and a worsening of the European balance of payments. The joint interests of the United States and Canada require that the capital flow from the former to the latter not be unduly restricted (the Canadian interest), and that it not result in a loss of gold reserves by the United States to Canada (the American interest). This joint interest can be served by co-ordinating management policies so that the capital flow and the Canadian current account are roughly in balance, and by Canada undertaking to hold any increments in reserves in dollars rather than gold. Such co-ordination, however, requires close consultation between the two countries, since the balance of payments between them is extremely volatile.

Turning to framework policies, it is equally self-evident

that there are a number of important areas in which co-ordination or joint action could bring significant improvement in the efficiency of operation of the two economies, and even more important, in the efficiency of their economic growth, to the mutual advantage of the two countries. All of these areas involve moving towards a continental rather than an individual national approach to economic organization and development planning, and specifically towards pooling, on some fair basis, the markets of the two countries for particular groups of products or services. The chief difficulty one encounters in discussing them is that essentially one is talking about the desirability of subordinating established policies of economic nationalism to the criteria of economic efficiency. Since Canadian economic nationalism is a highly sensitive factor that both Canadian and American officials have been schooled to treat with the tender solicitude reserved for immature adults, there is a general tendency for those who discuss this subject to concentrate their attention on new economic developments on which Canadian sentiment has not yet hardened into emotional irrationality, and in dealing with longer-standing issues, such as trade, to espouse solutions whose prime characteristic is that Canadian nationalism takes no risk of loss, no matter how economically irrational it is. The danger in this tendency is that of not cutting deeply or broadly enough into the spectrum of possibilities of joint planning; and I am sorry to have to criticize the Merchant-Heeney *Report* for skimming over some of these possibilities. As I have indicated on many occasions in the past, I believe that closer integration of the two economies into one continental economy would be beneficial to both countries, and would involve no loss of any Canadian nationalist objective worth pursuing. I have too much respect for the genuine worth of Canada to feel obliged to pamper nationalist insecurities by taking them more seriously than they deserve. However, I shall attempt to maintain an objective position, and confine myself to pointing out the main areas in which joint planning and action might produce substantial benefits for both parties.

The most obviously promising opportunity for joint planning is the reduction or elimination of the two sets of barriers to trade between themselves imposd by the countries. These barriers reduce the efficiency of resource use in both countries, though their impact is far greater on the Canadian than on the American economy. The Canadian tariff promotes small-scale, inefficient, and high-cost manufacturing, which had considerable difficulty in competing in world markets until about 1964, when the advantage of a devaluation combined with the presence of slack demand has apparently provided the ability and incentive to export. As is generally recognized, the reduction of these barriers would impose far more serious adjustment problems for Canada than for the United States, so that special arrangements would be necessary to cushion the adjustment of Canadian industry to the change.

The reduction of barriers to Canadian-American trade could be approached in a variety of ways; not all of these, however, are consistent with the two countries' obligations under GATT, nor would all be economically beneficial. The most practical approach consistent with GATT, and the one most likely to produce economically beneficial results, would be the formation of a free trade area between the two countries, on the lines of the Canadian-American Committee studies previously referred to. At present, however, considerable attention is being given in official circles in Canada to the alternative of individual arrangements for selected industries, similar to the recently-signed agreement on automotive products. There are even those in Ottawa who regard the automobile agreement as a model of what Canada can do by unilateral action to force the United States into economic integration on Canadian terms. I consider both these views—that the automotive agreement represents a desirable way of working towards free trade, and that the automobile case provides an exemplar for the exercise of Canadian power over the United States—to be extremely superficial, and the latter to be a dangerous self-delusion. The agreement is, on the Canadian side, in violation of the spirit of GATT, which proscribes subsidization of exports, and on the American side, in violation of the letter of GATT, which proscribes new preferential arrangements. On the basis of my reading of the history that led up to the agreement, the concurrence of the United States administration was an act of high statesmanship designed to save the Canadian Prime Minister from the embarrassment that would have ensued on the collapse of a beggar-my-neighbour policy motivated by petty nationalism; the results would very likely have been quite different had there been a different Canadian Prime Minister, a less charismatic American President, a less intransigeant French President to annoy the American administration, or the prospect of a bad year instead of a booming one for the American automobile industry. Apart from the political considerations, the piecemeal sectoral approach to freer trade has the great disadvantage that it requires a governmental guess about comparative advantage, in the absence of any reliable market evidence of where comparative advantage really lies.

Though the freeing of international trade in commodities is an obvious area in which joint planning promises substantial mutual benefits, it has been realized more and more that tariffs and other barriers to trade are only one aspect of the many ways in which national economic policies impede the exploitation of the advantages of economic integration. Specifically, it has become increasingly evident that some of the important sources of economic inefficiency attributable to national economic policies are policies that influence business costs or the availability of natural resources to consumers and producers. To be concrete, three particular sectors of economic activity have been held out in current discussion as promising substantial mutual gains from joint planning by Canada and the United States: the use of energy, the use of water resources, and the organization of transportation.

With respect to energy, the Merchant-Heeney *Report* concentrates on the possibilities of reducing the costs of the use of hydro-electric power through continental planning. These possibilities are particularly striking in the case of hydro power, because of the economies of scale in generation, the new technology of ultra-high-voltage transmission, and the peak-load problem associated with high fixed costs of generation and the wide fluctuation of demand over the day, which can be reduced by marrying demands from different time zones or from regions with different economic structures. Similar, though less spectacular, problems, however, arise with respect to all energy sources, since all of them tend to be localized in origin and to involve significant costs of transportation to the market. Consequently, governmentally-imposed barriers to marketing that oblige energy, or the materials required to produce it, to be transported to distant markets rather than nearby markets impose substantial costs— costs which could be eliminated by a continental rather than a national approach to the definition of markets.

The pooling of water resources on a continental basis is not presented as a promising area of joint planning in the Merchant-Heeney *Report*; but the question has become an urgent one as a consequence of the water shortage on the east coast of the United States.[3] There is no

---

[3]The question is discussed at some length in Stanley R. Tupper, "United States-Canadian Relations," *Congressional Record*, Sept. 28, 1965.

doubt that the water shortage is a problem that will have to be faced; on the other hand, any economist must be aware that much of the problem is a result of the failure to charge to consumers of water the economic cost of the water they consume and to polluters of water the economic value of the water resources they destroy, and that there are other ways of supplying more water than finding and piping new sources of fresh water, such as reclamation and the desalination of sea water. The possibility of substantial gain from a continental approach to water supply, such as that envisaged in the North American Water and Power Alliance (NAWAPA) scheme is therefore less obvious than appears at first sight. Nevertheless, Canada and the United States have enough water resources in common (most notably, the Great Lakes and Columbia River systems), and enough disparity between water availabilities and water demands, to make a joint approach to the water question eminently sensible.

The third area of potential benefit from joint planning is transportation. On this subject, the Merchant-Heeney *Report* confines itself to civil aviation, and argues the desirability of a continental pattern of air travel. To stop there, however, is merely to scratch the surface of the transportation problem and to confine attention to the conveniences of consumption rather than the needs of efficient production. While it is true that the national basis of air travel routing is extremely inconvenient for anyone who wants to travel between moderate-sized cities in the two countries, far more important sources of inefficiency are the national and east-west orientation of road and rail routes—which are the predominant medium for the international movement of goods—and the system for fixing freight rates, which discriminate against international trade. The importance of freight-rate formulas as a factor influencing international trade was a major discovery of the European Coal and Steel Community; and there would seem to be a strong *prima facie* case for a joint approach to the freight-rate question as a means of improving continental efficiency.

In my discussion so far, I have concentrated on the possibilities of joint planning by Canada and the United States. Now, I am obliged to consider the limitations of joint planning; and I shall conclude with a discussion of these.

My first observation, which is a brusquer and briefer version of much carefully worded wisdom contained in the Merchant-Heeney *Report*, is that joint planning is possible only to the extent that each partner has both an understanding of the other's world position and interests, and confidence in the stability of the other's behaviour. In this context, the greatest problem is that each partner tends to assume that history and propinquity give it an intuitive and automatic understanding of the other. This is untrue and dangerous. It is equally untrue and dangerous for both, because, though the United States tends to take Canada too much for granted, and particularly to ignore what is going on in Canadian opinion on the assumption that nothing can really go wrong up here, Canadians are prone to make the opposite error; to assume that American policy is made in random fashion, according to the views vociferated by various public figures, and to regard the United States as a blind giant whose company is dangerous but who can be terrified or cajoled into accepting policies against his own political and economic interests. This mutual misunderstanding is largely the result of difference in the systems of government between the two countries: the Canadian parliamentary system draws a clear distinction between what can be said in political debates and what can be said and done by the government in power; while the American system allows continual public debate over policy, with no clear distinction between those who make policy and those who criticize it. Nevertheless, it maintains a continuity of policy more consistent than is apparent to the outside observer of American political life. Progress in joint planning depends on recognition by the two partners of the real facts: recognition by Americans that Canadians are not simply Americans living in a small adjacent country and anxious to demonstrate their Americanism; and recognition by Canadians that Americans are not simply Canadians blessed by more numbers, money, and international power than they can handle.

My second, and concluding, observation is that even under the best of circumstances joint planning is no panacea for the problems of the two countries. There are genuine differences of national interests and objectives, which consultation can clarify but not resolve; in these cases, and agreement to disagree, rendered tolerable and acceptable by the cordiality of the over-all relationship, is the best that can be hoped for. Moreover, even with the ultimate in cordiality, there are limits to what planning can accomplish: for in democratic societies, planning is dependent on the co-operation of the planned; and in a number of areas of potential joint planning I have discussed, it is highly probable that either private enterprise or state and provincial governments will have their own dissident views on where the social interest lies.

II. BUSINESS

Towards a National
Science Policy

O. M. SOLANDT*

IT IS NOT POSSIBLE here to give a complete outline of a
national science policy, so I shall concentrate on a few of
the aspects of such a policy that seem peculiar to Canada.
A national science policy for this country requires careful
planning and is an area where the decisions that Canada
takes will be of more than passing interest to the United
States.

Since the Second World War, scientific research has
developed into a major industry in its own right, and the
rapid application of the results in the form of new products or processes has become one of the major forces in
industrial expansion. As the fostering of national economic
prosperity is one of the primary aims of most governments,
it follows that governments are becoming more and more
interested in how they spend their money on research.

*Chancellor of the University of Toronto, and Vice President, de
Havilland Aircraft (Canada) Limited.

They are becoming increasingly aware of the need to develop a well-thought-out policy for the use of science that will lead to detailed plans for action and will maximize the economic benefits of new scientific discoveries.

It is becoming apparent that no nation, however vast its resources and however successful its research, can pursue every avenue of scientific inquiry. Even the United States must be selective. It follows then that Canada, with about a tenth of the American resources, must be even more narrowly selective.

Fortunately, the broad outlines of a national science policy for Canada are fairly obvious. First in the field of fundamental research, we must seek to find money to provide good salaries and ample facilities for all the gifted people who are capable of doing first-class fundamental scientific research. If this definition is rigidly applied, the number to be supported will be well within our resources. In most cases, the equipment needed for fundamental research is quite modest, but where the facilities required are very expensive, we may sometimes have to be ruthless in our choice. Nothing but the best is good enough for fundamental research. It is far better to have one first-class institute at one university than to have mediocre facilities at three or four others, none of which will be adequate to attract and hold the best research workers. In a few cases we may have to take the unpalatable decision that what is needed is beyond our means. Satellite-launching facilities are a typical example.

Secondly, in applied research and development in industry, the broad outline of a policy is equally apparent: we should recognize the important new ideas arising in Canada as a potential resource of real value, and should do what we can to exploit our own originality. This will not always be possible because the resources required may strain our capacities, but in most cases it is lack of courage rather than lack of resources that leads to the exportation of our undeveloped ideas.

Thirdly, if we regard North America as a single economic unit, then we see that Canada represents a northern fringe having all the problems of a sparse population, great distances, relatively poor communication, a challenging climate, and a developing economy. Consequently, both technically and economically, Canada is quite different from most of the United States. In many cases, our physical needs are very different in detail. I am sure that there are many instances where equipment designed especially to meet Canadian needs could and would sell here—even if its price is relatively high because of small production runs.

In addition, many Canadians fail to realize that equipment developed to meet the needs of the Canadian frontier may well prove superior to American or European equipment when used in other frontier areas. For example, just after the War, the RCAF was faced with the problem of operating in northern Canada right up to the Pole in an area that was almost devoid of ground navigational aids. Therefore, great emphasis was put on developing navigational systems that could operate without ground stations. Several of the navigational units thus developed have found sale in many other countries where similar problems exist. The history of the de Havilland "Beaver" is another striking example. This aeroplane was designed to meet the needs of northern bush pilots in Canada and particularly of the Ontario Provincial Air Service. It successfully met the need in Canada for a rugged, simple, general utility, transport aircraft using short runways. It soon appeared that many other undeveloped areas in the world had a need for a similar plane. The "Beaver" is now operating in more than sixty countries in the world. It has been in production, with comparatively small design changes, for eighteen years, and is still selling. The same is true in several kinds of communications equipment. Systems designed to meet the needs of the Canadian hinterland have found ready markets in other parts of the world where similar problems exist.

From these and other considerations, the broad outline of a national science policy for Canada emerges. It could be briefly stated thus: (1) Give ample support to fundamental research in the universities. This will make Canada's contribution to scientific capital in the world. It will also serve as a training ground for pure and applied scientists of the future. (2) Encourage the entire scientific community to think of possible applications of the results of their work in strengthening the economy of Canada. (3) Applied research and development should be mainly in industry and should concentrate where possible on unique Canadian requirements. (4) Money available for major research facilities should not be fragmented, but should be used to build units of outstanding excellence. Where these deal with fundamental research, they should be housed in a university and operated for all the universities. Where they are operated by government, they must be in the closest touch with the universities and with industry. (5) Defence research, development, and production should all be planned to do as much to strengthen the commercial competence of Canadian industry as possible without sacrificing important defence needs.

If these principles are followed, we shall have evolved in Canada a strong scientific community, founded on good fundamental research in the universities, and resulting in strong, competent, manufacturing industries that can compete successfully in world markets. I believe that such a policy will particularly ensure success in competition with the United States because it automatically avoids head-on competition with their vast mass-producing industries. If we design specifically to meet Canadian requirements, we will, in most cases, be aiming at rather limited and specialized markets in which we can compete successfully with our larger friend south of the border. Thus, a national science policy of the kind that I have outlined will tend automatically to make Canadian and American aims complementary rather than strongly competitive. This should be good for both nations.

Energy Resources

J. W. KERR*

IT IS MY PURPOSE to make a few comments on planning for the effective use of our energy resources on a North American basis. Because of the significance of current planning, by Trans-Canada Pipe Lines Limited, to the future of the natural gas industry in the mid-western United States and in eastern Canada, I also propose to use our Great Lakes project as a specific example, or case history, of long-range international planning.

The reference to energy, in the Merchant-Heeney *Report*, seems to be particularly applicable to the basic

*Chairman and President, Trans-Canada Pipe Lines Limited, Toronto.

requirement for long-range planning in the energy industries on a continental basis. I quote from the energy section of the *Report*: "We have been impressed by the prospects of mutual benefit which might be realized in closer co-operation and co-ordination between our two countries in the production and distribution of energy. . . ." (p. 39.)

Co-operation between the United States and Canada is usually taken for granted by most people. However, when we remember that the population of our continent will probably double by the end of this century, we realize that practical co-operation and efficient planning are absolutely basic and fundamentally necessary if our combined resources are to be effective.

Over the years Canada's role as a catalyst and as a spokesman in international affairs has been recorded on many pages of history. Canadian statesmanship has been recognized on many occasions. However, Canada's role in marshalling our total continental resources is not fully appreciated. Without full and effective co-operation between Canada and the United States, a serious crisis in the development of both countries could easily occur. Planning is the process used to prevent such a crisis. It is not just a doctrine; it is an important tool. To be effective, this tool must be designed and adapted to the tasks for which it is to be used, always bearing in mind the general economic, social, political, cultural, and historical conditions under which it will operate.

Certainly the Canadian natural gas industry could not have prospered and progressed to its present importance in the economy without serious attention to the planning function. In the twenty years of the post-war period, natural gas has increased its share of the United States energy market from 13 per cent in 1945 to an estimated 35 per cent for 1965. Although relatively small volumes of natural gas have been available in the southwestern area of Ontario for many years, natural gas has been available throughout Canada in abundant volumes for only seven years. During that period, in spite of keen competition for the energy dollar, natural gas has increased its participation in the Canadian energy market from 9 per cent in 1958 to an estimated 18 per cent in 1965. It expects to supply 25 per cent of Canada's energy requirements by 1970. Acceptance of natural gas would not have developed to this significance in the energy spectrum if "Big-Inch" pipelines had not been planned and constructed on an international basis, with sales to the United States markets planned to supplement sales in Canada. With proper planning for the future natural gas resources in the western Canadian sedimentary basin can be developed on a continental basis in a way that will provide the most efficient and most economical use of this form of energy.

As the market-place across Canada has increased the incentive for exploration and drilling, huge reserves which exceed the requirements of present connected markets have been discovered and proven. These reserves are in our western Canadian sedimentary basin, comprising part of Saskatchewan, all of Alberta, northeastern British Columbia, the Yukon, and the Northwest Territories east to Hudson Bay. They have strategic importance for almost the entire North American continent. Wise use of these abundant and valuable reserves requires extensive forecasts of markets in both the United States and Canada. To be ready for the market, all developments in the energy business must be planned many years before they are needed. Fortunately, the energy business, and certainly the natural gas business, lends itself to long-term planning.

The flow of gas in North America back and forth across the 49th parallel is to be commended. The methods used here are being copied in planning for the marketing of newly discovered gas in Europe. Already the very prolific reserves of Dutch gas are being shared with neighbours of the Netherlands, and the pooling of this great energy source in the Benelux area and around the North Sea is being planned.

Although the Canadian natural gas industry has existed on a national scale for only a relatively short period of seven years, already it has nine interconnections with gas pipeline systems in the United States. These important international links in our economy are at Philipsburg, Quebec, on the Vermont border; in Ontario at Cornwall, Niagara Falls, and Windsor; at Emerson, Manitoba; at Aden and Cardston, Alberta; and at Kingsgate and Sumas, British Columbia. While some of these locations are little known, these connecting points serve to ensure lowest-cost natural gas service, continuity of service, and standby emergency facilities for millions of consumers on both sides of the international border. This flow of gas is an example of the type of co-operative planning by private industry, based upon governmental co-operation, that is so vital to the existence of the international neighbourhood in which we operate. While it is only a beginning, it is already a model for planning on a scale that is little known elsewhere in the world.

The Canadian natural gas industry is also pleased that its first composite effort to plan ahead was successful. In June, 1965, the Canadian Gas Association adopted the theme, "From now until 1970." This was consistent with the pattern set by the *First Annual Review* of the Economic Council of Canada. Each major function of our industry was comprehensively examined, and a sober prophecy of a healthy five years ahead was made—an instructive and thought-provoking experience. Such planning is fortunately being done by several other industries, and these efforts will surely be helpful to our national economy.

Planning on a continental scale was also involved in the plan to build a loop, or second natural gas line, from Alberta to Ontario and Quebec by taking the short-cut across Michigan, Wisconsin, and Minnesota. It is usually known as the Great Lakes Project. Geography, and not an artificial boundary line, is the deciding factor in this project. It is much the same as the New York Central Railroad cutting across the Niagara Peninsula from Niagara to Windsor for its direct express line from New York City to Chicago. The people of Windsor and Detroit have long been familiar with this common-sense application of Canadian-American co-operation. The project is the joint effort of Trans-Canada Pipe Lines Limited and the American Natural Gas Company of Detroit. The joint planning and preliminary engineering of the project began four years ago and the first breaking of ground, subject to the approval of both governments, will begin next summer when the first phase of the project is scheduled to be built in Michigan. The balance of this $200 million project is estimated for completion in 1967.

To make this project possible, the relationship of western Canada's natural gas reserves to the total North American market was studied in great detail. The long-term requirements for gas of major distribution companies were examined carefully; the supply and sales data of adjacent American pipelines were fully analysed; and the feasibility of a complete new $1 billion pipeline from west to east was compared with planned additions to the existing Trans-Canada system. Forecasts for the potential of competing fuels were prepared, so that a full appraisal of the energy supply and market picture on a long-term basis could be considered. Several alternate routes for the pipe-line were examined, including routes south of Lake Michigan through various sections of Wisconsin and Michigan, and underground storage possibilities in the market area were examined.

Initially Trans-Canada was faced with the possibility of proceeding with no American partner and without sales to United States markets from the proposed new pipeline system. However, after much negotiation, which is really part of the planning process, the American Natural Gas Company became a joint partner and, in return, committed itself to purchase substantial volumes of Canadian gas from the new pipeline. This improved the feasibility of the project in a substantial manner and proved the value of joint planning and co-operative effort by modifying the project to benefit both companies.

Trans-Canada also is planning a new "Big-Inch" system from northern Alberta in approximately a straight line through Saskatchewan. Subject to proof of gas reserves and governmental approval, Trans-Canada will, by 1968, have the equivalent of a complete new system from the Alberta gas fields, south of the Great Lakes, to the eastern Canadian market. From a security of service point of view, this is most significant. The economies of the route south of Lake Superior and Lake Huron will also be most beneficial to eastern Canadian consumers.

In the next twenty years the North American energy market will require more fossil fuel, in the form of oil, gas, or petroleum liquids, than was discovered in North America in the century before 1965. This calls for a degree of planning and advance construction of facilities that staggers the imagination. We feel that private enterprise has the main burden of this planning and must take the initiative in convincing the governments concerned that provision for this type of growth must be started now and pushed along on a continuous basis. It is not a situation where we can wait for the sudden emergence of excess demand before the plans for construction are made.

All consumers of energy, from the home owner who uses energy for light, for cooking, and for heat, to the large industrial user, have a vital stake in this question. They have a right to expect that scientific and economic planning will be done by all groups, both public and private, which are involved in the problem. Maximum efficiency, improved productivity, conservation of capital, and lowest possible cost must be the goals. The natural gas industry on both sides of the border is planning and building on the basis that these criteria will prevail.

Private Planning in the Public Interest

GROVER W. ENSLEY*

As ONE WITH YEARS in the government service and, more recently, in private business, I have had the opportunity to observe the growing importance of planning and co-operation within and between both areas. I should like

*Executive Vice President of the National Association of Mutual Savings Banks, New York.

to comment now on some aspects of business planning in the United States, as a prelude to the consideration of an expanded role for private business planning in the achievement of broad social and economic goals. Planning to meet the challenge of automation is one obvious area of intense business concern and participation, but the role of business can, and should, be even broader. There is, it seems to me, a vast opportunity open to the private sector of a mixed economy such as that of the United States or Canada—an opportunity to participate in planning the quality and direction of national life for generations to come.

The increasingly important role of business economists and of business planning in the over-all managerial function, both in the area of short-range forecasting of the business cycle and of long-range corporate strategic planning, reflects the tremendous growth in the absolute size and complexity of the economy and of individual business organizations, the accelerating pace of technological change and innovation, and the greatly expanded role of government in the economic area. The sheer size of the American economy and its steady and spectacular growth since the dark days of depression in the 1930's need little elaboration; nor does the increasing complexity that growth has brought to the structure of the economy and to the individual firm.

Closely related to these developments, and to the growth of business planning in the United States, is the continuing technological revolution that has contributed so greatly to the growth, complexity, and rapidity of change that characterize the modern American economy. By increasing the uncertainty of the future and by accelerating change, technological advances have greatly increased the need for planning and made the process considerably more difficult.

But there is another side of the technological coin. Electronic data processing, for example, has already contributed significantly to more efficient business planning. In the future its role will grow in importance. Many government and business statistical programs have already been, or are in the process of being, automated. And the high speed and flexibility of the computer not only will permit more rapid, efficient, and extensive statistical collection and reporting, but will also permit more sophisticated utilization of these statistics by planners.

The extensive statistical services provided by the federal government, of course, reflect its sharply expanded role in virtually all areas of economic activity. Most obvious, perhaps, is the rise in federal spending. But the influence of the federal government in the modern, mixed economy extends far beyond the spending area. Anti-trust and regulatory activity, and monetary and debt management policies have far-reaching effects on the economy and on private business decisions. More recently, our federal government's concept of wage-price guidelines and its voluntary balance of payments program have enlarged the area of contact between the government and private sectors.

Government has always been involved in the economic affairs of the nation to some extent. But under the stress of the Depression and the Second World War, its role was sharply expanded. Since the War, the influence of the federal government in the United States has been expanded still further, under the mandate of the Employment Act of 1946, to promote maximum employment, production, and purchasing power. The Employment Act, in addition to giving formal recognition to the federal government's assumption of responsibility for promoting broad national goals in the economic area—thus increasing the need for private knowledge of government activities—has, as I have indicated, also greatly enhanced the ability of private business to plan for the future. The Act established, in the Office of the President, the Council of Economic Advisers, and in Congress, the Joint Economic Committee. In accordance with their responsibilities under the Act, both bodies have made significant contributions to the development of economic statistics, to new analytical techniques, and to economic education generally.

In a study published by the Joint Economic Committee in 1954 the concept of the gap between actual and potential GNP was first developed. It was also during this period that the Joint Committee began publication of *Economic Indicators*, a monthly pamphlet prepared by the Council of Economic Advisers summarizing important economic indicators in a concise, readable and readily accessible form. And it was during this period that the Joint Economic Committee undertook the first governmental examination of the emerging phenomenon of automation and its implications for the economy, summarizing its findings and recommendations in a report entitled *Automation and Technological Change*.

The dramatic post-war improvement in the quality and scope of statistical programs and economic investigations is still going on as the era of the Employment Act approaches the end of its second decade. As a result, today, a vast amount of current and readily accessible information lies at the disposal of business and government planners. In a very real sense, it is the availability of such information and the development of automation and modern statistical and econometric techniques that has enabled the free-market, mixed economy of the United States to achieve a level of national wealth and individual income unmatched in the history of nations. Today, more than ever before, economic information is truly the lifeline of growth and progress, the vital link connecting and co-ordinating the autonomous decisions of the sixty million consumer units, five million business units and more than ninety thousand governmental units that comprise the complex and interrelated economy of the United States.

The development of government growth and stabilization policies since the 1930's, and the related expansion of vital economic information, illustrate how government in the United States has become not a rival but a major ally of private business in making a capitalist, market economy function efficiently in today's complex world. Indeed, the great beauty of such a system is its flexibility—its ability to function under normal circumstances at close to full-employment levels.

The ready availability of vital information—from such diverse sources as the federal budget, surveys of business and consumer spending plans, industry input-output tables and hundreds of other economic series—has built a self-correcting, co-ordinating mechanism into the American economy. Given the availability of such information, and the speed of computers, plans and models of economic behaviour can constantly be changed and revised in the light of new information. Imbalances between economic sectors and emerging trends that could have led to disastrous consequences in earlier days can now more readily be recognized and corrected in time.

This is not to say that we have reached the millenium. A great deal still remains to be done to improve our economic information system. We should also remember that economic models and mathematical relationships, while useful tools to the planner, cannot provide automatic answers to problems. Informed, individual judgement will still provide the basis of planning. I think one of the great errors of Soviet planning has been the disregard of the essential human equation in their search for scientific, mathematical answers to the problems of production and resource allocation. In this regard, it will be interesting to see how far recent Soviet moves toward the market test will be carried, and indeed, whether they can be reversed once started.

So far, I have discussed the impact of government upon the development of private business planning in the United States, particularly with regard to the policies and statistical programs growing out of the Employment Act of 1946. I should now like to shift the focus of discussion to the effect that private business planning could, and I believe should, have upon the achievement of national goals enumerated or implied in the Employment Act. In short, I should like to talk about the potential of private planning in the public interest, particularly with respect to automation.

Business must recognize that it too has a responsibility for achieving national goals. The real question is not whether plans will be made to achieve national goals, but rather who will do the planning. I submit that in mixed economies, such as those of the United States and Canada, there is a large area for private business planning and participation in the building of the "Great Society."

Robert Austin, a professor at the Harvard Business School and a director of several business firms, has advanced the thesis that a large share of social change can be traced to radical technological changes instituted by business, and that the failure of business to foresee the social effects of its actions has inevitably led to a sharp expansion of government activity. In Mr. Austin's words:

The true responsibility of business leadership is to make some appraisal of the social effects flowing from its strategic policy decisions and technological advances. . . . Having made some judgement as to the social effects of its activities, business must then make the effort to think beyond the economic and see what kind of action should be taken, and by whom, to meet the problems of social change.

The rise of automation is one such technological advance that has had, and will increasingly have, a tremendous impact on national life in the United States and other countries. And, in this regard, Professor Austin's emphasis on the social responsibility of business was expressed almost a decade earlier by the Joint Economic Committee's Report on *Automation and Technological Change*. The *Report* stressed that, "The genius and industry which create and boast of 'thinking machines' cannot and ought not to be allowed to shift all of the problems created by them to the shoulders of Government and labor." Labour, management, and government all recognize the long-run benefits to progress and efficiency inherent in automation. We must be equally aware of the human and social costs involved. For the displaced worker, particularly the older worker, these costs can be very great indeed. In my opinion, one of the greatest challenges today is finding a way to reconcile the drive for progress and efficiency with the need for orderly and humane adjustment to rapid change. This is no easy task.

In the United States, a significant share of the federal government's attention is being directed towards problems of structural unemployment, poverty and depressed geographic areas—problems caused or aggravated by automation and technological change, and by the lack of requisite skills and education of a large segment of the population. The Manpower Development and Training Act, the Employment Opportunity Act, the Vocational Education Act, the Economic Opportunity Act, the Public Works and Economic Development Act, the Appalachian Regional Development Act, and the Elementary and Secondary Education Act are some of the important government measures enacted in the past two years to deal with important problems of training, education, labour mobility, and poverty.

Private business, too, is thinking and acting upon the broader implications of automation and technological change. In my opinion, these efforts should be intensified. In particular, there should be increased consultation and co-operation between business and labour to cushion the short-run dislocations arising from the introduction of automation. Every effort must be made to deal in a rational manner with the problems created by automation —that is, by planning. Business plans calling for the introduction of automation should incorporate provisions for retraining or relocation programs and should provide for the active participation of labour in such efforts. As the Joint Economic Committee stated in 1955, "Industry, and management for its part, must be prepared to accept the human costs of displacement and retraining as charges against the savings from the introduction of automation . . . by careful planning and scheduling, the adjustments of workers and the stoppage of employment can be minimized. . . ."

Business has become familiar with the techniques and theory of planning, and it has the resources to make its plans effective. In active partnership and co-operation with government, labour and other interested groups, increased business participation in achieving broad social and economic goals will act to further another basic goal —the preservation of freedom and self-reliance in national life. In the words of Alfred North Whitehead, "The great society is the one in which businessmen think greatly of their function."

Detroit Edison's
Approach to Planning

WALKER L. CISLER*

As is true for other similar companies serving their respective areas, the Detroit Edison Company has the responsibility of providing dependable electric service throughout 7,600 square miles in southeastern Michigan. This area represents only about 13 per cent of the land area of the state, yet in it live and work about 4.5 million people, more than half the population of Michigan. There has never been a shortage of electric energy in the area, even during the years of the Second World War when exceptional loads were placed upon industrial production capacity in the Detroit metropolitan area. During its more than sixty-two years of corporate entity, Detroit Edison has always had to foresee and meet the increasing demand for electric energy in Detroit, which grew rapidly during the early automotive years, during the First World War, and recently, has been expanding rapidly once again. The availability of sufficient and dependable electric energy does not come about by mere chance. We have had to look ahead, determine the characteristics of foreseeable growth, and then plan additions to generation, transmission, and distribution facilities accordingly.

The need for business planning is characteristic of the

*Chairman of the Board, the Detroit Edison Company.

electric energy industry. The investor-owned electric companies, representing some 75 per cent of electric-power generation in the United States, have a capital investment of about 60 billion dollars, the largest investment of any industry in the nation. It is presently increasing at the rate of more than 4 billion a year and this rate of investment will accelerate in the future.

Detroit Edison represents a capital investment of about 1.3 billion and some 95 per cent of this is in fixed assets. We must plan ahead accurately enough so that generating capacity will always be sufficient, with an adequate reserve margin. If there is too much reserve capacity, it stands idle while the carrying charges continue. Both for reasons of good service and economy in the utilization of investment, we must plan ahead most thoughtfully. Some of the factors which we must consider in making our plans are: economic trends in the area and in the nation in general; population growth and movement to suburbs and new communities; trends in residential, commercial and industrial use of electric energy; plans for highway development and urban renewal. On the basis of such factors we determine construction needs, basic energy requirements, rate structure, and financial plans.

Our forecasts can be made quite accurately up to five years ahead, with projections for ten and twenty years, subject to revision every so often. We seek to have four to five years of lead-time in designing and building new generating facilities. Almost as much lead-time is required to plan transmission lines, to secure rights of way and to do the actual construction. Because generating facilities, transmission lines, switching stations, substations and distribution networks are costly to build and more costly to change at later dates, sound business planning is essential. There must be proper recognition also of aesthetic values and public acceptance.

In recent years, I have felt the need for the company to

engage in an even more extensive and longer-range study of total economic growth trends in our service area. Such matters are in turn related to the economic growth of the Great Lakes area, including adjacent areas of Ontario and the northern part of Ohio. The study which we have begun extends from Milwaukee and Chicago to the west, to Toledo, Cleveland, Pittsburgh, and Toronto to the south and east. It is a five-year study which is being made in co-operation with Wayne State University, well known as a centre for urban planning. The study draws upon the technical resources of Doxiadis Associates, Inc., of Athens, Greece, an organization that has engaged in urban and regional planning and development in twenty-three countries on four continents. Dr. Constantinos Doxiadis has become world famous as an engineer, architect, and urban planner, and agrees that there is a serious need for understanding the complex problems of economic growth, population increase, and urban development, and emphasizes the need to do this sufficiently in advance.

By the end of this century world population may well double from the present 3.3 billion people to 6 billion or more. Each new individual requires an endowment of energy, natural resources, employment, a home and a community in which to live, a place in life. Unless men plan more objectively in the future than they have in the past, the basic factors of urban life—environment, transportation, housing, services, recreation, and culture—may fall far short of what should be provided.

A few years ago I asked Dr. Doxiadis whether a very thorough and long-range study of the area around Detroit could be undertaken. I felt that such a study would provide important new guidelines for the growth of Detroit Edison and other companies, and that it would serve the needs of planning authorities and all who took an interest in the advancement of human as well as economic values.

In 1964 the study was begun. It concerns the physical,

organizational, economic, and human trends across more than 20,000 square miles, including 35 of the 83 counties in Michigan, 9 counties in Ohio and 3 in Ontario. This broad approach is necessary because community, state, and national boundaries do not necessarily define economic and human boundaries.

Phase I in the study was completed in September 1965. The purpose of this phase was to gather all available data on past and present growth patterns. As many as one hundred and fifty aspects of the area have been studied and reduced to maps and charts, showing graphically the trends that are at work. A report on Phase I will be published soon.

Phase II has begun and will continue through most of 1966. This will determine how the study should proceed in depth and it will identify the gaps that are apparent in long-range area planning.

Phase III will carry on into 1970, developing a clear picture of where the area is going and what kinds of forward planning are necessary between 1970 and the year 2000. Though our interest extends well into the twenty-first century, the immediate concern is with the period of the next thirty to thirty-five years—certainly not a long period in corporate and regional planning, or even in a lifetime.

In December 1965, Dr. Doxiadis presented the program and preliminary results to leaders in government, business, education, finance, and services from Milwaukee to Pittsburgh. Results of the study to date suggested that growth during the next thirty-five years will have little resemblance to growth in the past. By the year 2000 the population of southeastern Michigan is expected to increase from the present 4.5 million to perhaps more than 10 million people. Population and construction of all kinds will probably double everything that has been done since Detroit was founded some two hundred and sixty-four years ago. At present in the Detroit Edison service area about 16 per cent of the land is urbanized. By the year 2000 we feel more than 50 per cent will be urbanized. The trend maps show an interesting pattern of growth around the principal cities. Each city is being surrounded by ever more extensive satellite suburbs. Urbanization is increasing along the main highways between cities, foreshadowing the denser urbanization that will in time completely connect many cities in the future.

Dr. Doxiadis foresees a truly remarkable economic growth and urbanization from Milwaukee and Chicago to Detroit, and then from Detroit in one direction across Ontario to Toronto and Buffalo and in a somewhat different direction from Detroit to Cleveland and Pittsburgh. He believes that in the next century or sooner a supercity or megalopolis will develop in this area, exceeding in time the urbanization that now extends along the Atlantic seaboard from Boston past Washington. He points out that the eastern megalopolis is hemmed in somewhat by the Appalachian Mountains, whereas there is abundant level land around the southern Great Lakes area—a location that is very near to major marketing areas, that has access to plentiful natural resources, and the largest resource of fresh water on the continent. In people, in training, in engineering and management skills, in standing enterprises, and educational facilities we have an excellent start toward such a development.

The results of the study will be brought into the advance planning of Detroit Edison, and these results will be so comprehensive that we should be able to plan more effectively than ever before. One of the tasks of our management will be to translate these trends and guidelines into corporate planning, into people, into facilities, and into investment requirements. In many ways this will be a new way of thinking about the relationships of the company to the area it serves.

The study will be equally helpful to others like ourselves, to planning groups, to industry, education, government and civic development. No study just like this has been undertaken elsewhere and it is possible that other cities in Canada and the United States will find the approach useful. As the study progresses the results will be made available to all who have a need for the data. Along the way, the co-operation of communities, organizations, and others will be necessary and most welcome. The results of the study should be as significant for Windsor and Ontario as they will be for the sister cities in the United States. In the middle of the great urbanization that is foreseen are the cities of Detroit and Windsor.

Basically the purpose of the study is to determine what has happened in the past to this area and what made it happen. From these guidelines we can foresee what may happen in the future. With such knowledge the questions of planning for the best course of development and for the most efficient facilities to serve people come to the forefront. Dr. Doxiadis is giving much personal attention to this aspect of the study—and this is the aspect that will depend upon the decisions of the public at large.

Cities in the past have mostly grown haphazardly, somewhat like Topsy, and all too often the net results have not been favourable to human aspirations. Dr. Doxiadis believes that we should not wait to see what happens and then try to correct shortcomings. He thinks urbanization should be planned far ahead, using all of our modern technological and intellectual resources. In the long run this is much less expensive and much more logical.

The study is an example of the close relationship in the economic affairs and aspirations of our two nations and a symbol of the kind of co-operation in many fields that we must seek as we go along the way together.

III. LABOUR

Labour and Social Planning

JOSEPH D. KEENAN*

IT IS VERY GRATIFYING to me that, more and more, labour is being called upon to take part in the processes of economic and social planning. It has not always been this way. In fact there was a time when, in the opinion of many other groups, labour proposed something it could only lead to economic ruin and must be rejected out of hand. Labour in turn, let me add, was not always blameless in its attitudes towards other groups. It is a sign of maturity on all sides that we are beginning to realize our common interests and objectives and to recognize the need for planning and working together in meeting them.

In a special way we welcome the opportunity to participate in the area of Canadian-American planning, for the labour organizations of our two countries have had a close association over the years. More than four-fifths of the

*International Secretary, International Brotherhood of Electrical Workers, Washington.

affiliates of the Canadian Labour Congress are members of international unions affiliated with the AFL-CIO, as well as with the CLC.

My own union, the International Brotherhood of Electrical Workers, was just eight years old in 1899 when the first Canadian electrical workers joined our Brotherhood. The relationship that we in the United States have had with Canada through this association has given us an insight into the differences and disagreements that are bound to arise between us. It has also shown us very clearly how tightly bound together are our mutual interests, our goals, our security, and our futures.

It is gratifying to me, too, that more groups in our society are recognizing the need for co-ordinated planning on a large scale to achieve our ideals. This also has not always been the case. In a free-market economy, many people tended to equate planning with socialism, and socialism with serfdom. Each new attempt at planning was said to take us farther along the road to socialism, but I do not look at it in this way. I think the proper word is "socialization," in the sense that it means adapting our resources to social needs or uses. This obviously must involve the government. But the American labour movement believes very strongly that government, which is the instrument of the people, should use its powers to attack and to help solve the people's problems.

Labour was one of the first groups to stress the need for co-ordinated planning by labour, the business community, government, educators, and other responsible groups. We watched developments in our society and saw their potential impact on people, as individuals and as groups. We called for careful study and advance planning to channel these developments in the right direction—planning to make sure that they would increase the well-being of people, not cause hardship.

Labour was the first to call attention to the threats of automation, at a time when others were saying there was nothing to worry about, that automation could bring nothing but good. We agreed with most of what was said about the potential benefits of automation. But we saw the problems it posed, and called for careful study and planning to help guide it in the direction it must go for human betterment. We were accused of being gloom merchants, of trying to block progress. This was not true. We saw what was happening to people and we believed, as we do now, that the test of progress is, not how quickly and cheaply we produce things but the effect on the way people live. Progress involves improving their economic security and their ability to provide good homes and a good education for their children.

Now that automation, with its threats and promises, is receiving widespread attention the need for planning has become painfully evident. Our administrators are faced with some extremely important decisions in determining the character and the future course of our nations. In setting our goals, and in devising ways to reach them, trade unions must play a major role. Labour, as one of North America's free institutions and the largest single group in our society, can make a significant contribution toward the solution of the critical and perplexing domestic and international problems facing us. Just about every occupational, racial, regional, and age group in our society is found within the framework of the labour movement. The potential is obvious. The labour movement could and should be a prime force in building a dynamic society dedicated to human values.

The scope of labour's representation is important in connection with planning processes. Sound planning requires the participation and guidance of scientists and experts. But, if it is to fulfil its obligations, it also requires popular participation and support. Planning cannot be regarded as the province of a special, remote group of experts making decisions in private and then imposing their plans on the public, with assurances that what is done is all for their own good.

The purpose of planning must be to advance the common good. And so it must be intimately associated with the people. It is in this area that labour, as representative of such a large mass of people, can make a most important contribution. Unions, so closely attuned to the needs of the people, have helped to assure that the basic values of our society are widely diffused. This we will continue to do, starting with the planning process.

In all of the planning, in working out specific goals and in searching for solutions, labour will keep emphasizing the fact that our basic concern is for people. In all of the necessary surveys, statistics, projections, and theories we must not lose sight of the individual. Our human resources are still our most valuable resources. And in creating a framework of policies and programs, we cannot afford to overlook or underestimate the many social problems involved. In other words, economic planning cannot be set apart from social and cultural planning; they are vital to each other.

A free, active, progressive trade union stands for a free, active, progressive country. In the field of social planning, I feel that labour has been far ahead of most other groups. I have already mentioned our concern over automation and its social impact. There are many other areas of concern, such as Medicare, for which we fought for twenty years, and housing. We have been calling for decent homes for low-income groups for more than three decades, and have felt that a nation which approved subsidies for farmers, for magazines and newspapers, and for numerous other groups could well invest in rent subsidies to provide decent homes for those who could not afford them otherwise. We also saw the need for planning and action in the area of mass transportation, and supported a bill more than ten years ago that was vetoed by the administration on the grounds that more information and planning was needed.

Some of the things we pointed out a need for have now been achieved. But so much more remains to be done. Our nations have prospered, but too many people have not shared in that prosperity. I read recently that there are something like 90,000 millionaires in the United States now. This is seven times as many as there were in 1948. Surely a nation that can produce 90,000 millionaires can also do something more effective to reduce unemployment, to conquer poverty and to improve the lot of less fortunate people.

Providing jobs and using all our resources to meet human needs are the fundamental challenges facing us. We have been telling the government that unemployment can be reduced simply by filling the nation's needs—the need for more schools, hospitals, and other institutions; the need for better health facilities; the need to improve our cities, and so on. We know that in the United States we can put people to work by meeting needs that ought to be met anyway. I am sure the same thing is true in Canada.

Meeting our fundamental challenges has to involve planning on a larger scale than ever before. It has to involve government action. Labour realizes this, and welcomes it. We want to be a part of it, because we feel we have a vital contribution to make. We realize, too, the responsibilities that planning places on us and we have been preparing ourselves for them. For example, we have been reaching out in new directions in our leadership training programs, to increase the depth of wisdom, awareness, and understanding of today's trade union leaders; and to give them a deeper insight into our society and the forces that are acting upon it.

We know that greater economic planning will have an effect on free collective bargaining requiring a greater maturity on the part of both labour and management, and more areas for common action. Labour-management relations will change, but as the government becomes more active in establishing or administering programs and policies to meet our goals, we must guard against any threats to free bargaining. It is an institution which has served us well. It is mature and flexible enough now to continue serving our nations well in the changing conditions of today and of the future.

Yet at a time when labour's contribution to planning and achieving a better society is so important, we find the labour movement still must defend itself from continuing attacks by those who would destroy our trade unions as free institutions. The problems that we are called upon to solve are increasingly complex. A weakening of free unions and of the free collective-bargaining structure could well have results quite contrary to the public interest.

Let us plan for the future in an atmosphere of mutual trust and understanding.

Labour Planning

DONALD MACDONALD*

FADDISM IS TO BE FOUND in economics as in other human interests and activities. Thus, for example, in the last few years we have seen a sudden preoccupation with automation and cybernation. We seem suddenly to have discovered—or perhaps more accurately rediscovered—poverty. More recently, economic planning and manpower policies have come to the fore as popular terms which have also captured the imagination of at least the more sophisticated members of the public and the politicians.

It strikes me as somewhat ironic that economic events which have long been matters requiring public attention, but which have been altogether too much neglected, should, quite suddenly, successfully compete for headline attention with political scandals and other popular reading matter. Poverty is as old as civilization itself. Automation, which I include with technological change generally, has confronted industry and working people since the beginnings of the industrial revolution. Consideration of economic planning and of its consequential manpower problems has arrived, in my opinion, much later than it should have done in an industrial complex as fully developed as our own. Hence my seemingly jaundiced

*Secretary-Treasurer, Canadian Labour Congress, Ottawa.

approach to a subject whose importance cannot be too much emphasized.

I come to you with an unabashedly subjective viewpoint. Not for me the necessarily disinterested approach of the social scientist. I am a labour leader, and have been one for many years. As such, I see the subject you have asked me to speak on today through the eyes of my constituency, the working people of Canada. For them, the long-range point of view holds little attraction. Subject as they are to the uncertainties and the insecurity which are almost a daily experience, what they want are assurances not for the next year, or the year after that, but for next week. If this seems short-sighted to you, I ask you to review in your minds the nature of their contract of service. If a man can be laid off on an hour's notice, or a week's notice, and if he has no assurance from one week to the next that his employment will continue, surely it is asking too much of him to project himself far into the future. In the long run, as Lord Keynes has so aptly said, and as everyone has so often repeated, we shall all be dead.

It will be argued, however, that there are a great many economic problems which cannot be solved by next week nor, for that matter, by next year. In that case, I am bound to say in reply, the sooner we get moving the better. We simply cannot afford to allow too many next weeks to go by without anything happening except as the result of the seemingly impersonal activities of the market. We must give the forces of the market-place direction, deliberately and positively. This is what I would understand by economic planning.

What are the assumptions I am bound to make in order to give a discussion of labour planning some meaning? I think, first of all, I must assume not only a dynamic

economy, but a public policy which states, in effect, that
the economy must continue to be expansionary in terms
of capital investment, in both the public and the private
sectors. I assume that the same policy will seek to reach
and to maintain a level of employment which is ordinarily
described as full employment. I assume furthermore that
the benefits of so dynamic an economy will be spread out
not only in terms of dividends or capital savings for further
investment, but also among the working population
generally so that there is an all-pervasive increase in living
standards, including also those who are too old or too
young to work, or who, for other reasons, are not in the
labour market.

I do not think this sounds utopian. I think these are
eminently legitimate and realizable objectives in an
economy such as ours. The assumptions I have made do
not come out of some imaginary situation, but represent
goals which have already been achieved in the non-
communist countries of northwestern Europe.

But the problems of automation and manpower disposition cannot wait for the realization of these goals.
They are with us now and must be solved, not when
economic planning has fulfilled its purpose, but as part of
the process of such planning. We are faced today with a
series of interrelated problems. One, which I would place
high on the list in terms of importance, is the failure of
our economy to provide for effective demand, which
reflects itself in our current preoccupation with poverty.

One of the obvious causes of our persistent unemployment is the lack of adequate purchasing power among
considerable segments of the working force and among
those who must rely on transfer payments, such as the
aged, the disabled, the unemployed, and others in similar
circumstances. To provide them with a greater measure

of income maintenance is, at the same time, to make a substantial contribution to the problem of labour planning, to the extent that such planning means the provision of jobs and the prosperity of those industries which cater to the satisfaction of consumer needs.

More obviously related to labour planning is the question of technological change. I prefer this term to automation, since I think the former is more comprehensive in its scope and sets out the problem more clearly. Placed in its simplest terms, technological innovation has had a long-term tendency to displace workers from their jobs and, at the same time, to render their particular skills obsolete.

Automation, in the more technically exact definition of the term (which I need not go into here), has tended to point up this tendency and to hasten the process of redundancy and skill obsolescence. If this is coupled with a disposition on the part of investors to relocate plants at the time the improved equipment is installed, the problem is compounded. Again, if there is a tendency, as indeed there is, for capital to concentrate very largely in the two central provinces of Canada, and in only certain parts of these provinces, the problem is complicated further, since we are inevitably aware of the existence of surplus labour not only in the Atlantic provinces, but in parts of the very provinces which show the greatest economic activity.

Labour planning is thus confronted by a triple problem: in the first instance, technological displacement; in the second, the disappearance of marketable skills in the case of those so displaced; in the third, the geographic distances between those who have their labour power to offer and those who might be in a position to purchase it.

For some generations it has been our practice in Canada to solve shortages of skilled workers by the easy expedient of importing them as immigrants. What our employers did, in effect, was to obtain such workers at the expense of fellow-employers in Europe and elsewhere. The full employment which now exists in most of western Europe has done very much to shut off this easy access to skilled workers. The increased tempo of technological change has confronted us with the fact of considerable numbers of semi-skilled and unskilled workers whose labour power is useless in its present form. The entrance of a large crop of adolescents into the labour market, many of them also with limited skills and certainly with no experience, has underlined the problem.

Labour planning is a complex of manpower policies which together must spell out an effective answer to those problems which I have so briefly sketched out. I cannot conceive of any form of labour planning which is not concretely based on a thorough and an on-going knowledge of the labour market, both present and future, in so far as it is humanly possible to project into the future. This should be the basic purpose of an institution such as the National Employment Service, to which the term National Manpower Service might be more appropriately given.

It is not enough for the employment service, whatever its title, merely to engage in the now familiar routine of providing a day-by-day placement service. It must engage in labour-market research to anticipate labour needs in terms of numbers, occupations, and locations. It must be equipped not only to make such projections based on sophisticated survey methods, but to prepare to serve both employers and employees in meeting the changing needs of the labour market.

This involves, first of all, a working knowledge of the direction in which industrial and technological investment is likely to go. Will there be new plants of the same kind as before and requiring the same type of labour? Will those plants be in the same place as before, or will they be located elsewhere? Will the new plants contain new kinds of production facilities calling for new types of labour? Will there be an adequate supply of labour—the right kind of labour—wherever the plants are located? Will it be possible to encourage capital to invest where there is labour, or must labour follow capital? What is the scope for on-the-job training, and what is the role of the educational system in terms of vocational needs and opportunities? How is labour mobility to be made effective, not only from the point of view of the would-be-employer, but in terms of the human needs of the would-be-employee? I submit to you that these are the kinds of questions which must become grist in the mill of any national manpower service in an industrialized country like ours. I put it to you also that we have yet to develop an instrument which can provide answers to these questions, not as an intellectual exercise but as a practical and effective program.

In looking at the Canadian manpower scene, we are bound to be struck by the fact that there seem to be answers to most, if not all, of the questions I have just suggested. Our National Employment Service has only recently been taken out of the Unemployment Insurance Commission, where it had had an uneasy existence, and has been placed directly within the Department of Labour. We have spent some hundreds of millions of dollars on vocational schools and institutes. Mobility grants and loans have become available to encourage unemployed workers to move where jobs are to be had. Fiscal incentives are provided to employers to locate in depressed areas. A manpower consultative service has been established to study the effects of technological change on employment. The Economic Council of Canada has been charged with the task of suggesting policies leading to the kind of dynamic economy to which I referred earlier. Surely each one of these is commendable in itself, at least on paper. But the question arises whether each is satisfactory in itself, and also whether the whole is greater than the sum of its parts. I believe that we have reason to think that neither is the case.

There is no clear evidence, as yet, to indicate that the National Employment Service will, in fact, become a national manpower service, engaged in short- and long-range labour-market surveys, administering a highly sophisticated employment service, giving guidance to employers and to employees as to the developments taking place in the labour market, and so on. Perhaps it is too early to make this kind of critical appraisal but, unfortunately, I have no evidence as yet that the National Employment Service is being converted, or at least expanded, to assume this very fundamental role in the framework of labour planning.

There is no room for debate about the desirability of an extended program of comprehensive facilities for vocational training and retraining. It has been suggested that where at one time a worker might expect to stay on the same kind of job his whole working life, technological changes are now occurring with such rapidity that he may have to change his job perhaps five times in his working life. I want to make it clear that I am not referring to changes of employers, but to changes in job content. In other words, he may have to relearn and re-equip himself for work several times between his entry in to the labour market as a youth and his final retirement.

Accordingly, if our vocational institutions are to have any vital meaning, they must be geared to a labour market which is in a constant state of flux in terms of occupational requirements. It is not only a matter of upgrading skills, which is right now a major preoccupation, and rightly so, but of regrading. I submit to you that vocational training cannot be unrelated to national manpower policies. Regardless of the constitutional divisions of this country and the almost parochial approach to labour markets, if we are to have a viable national economy, we are bound to integrate training and retraining programs with manpower policies generally.

Labour mobility presents special problems because labour is not merely a commodity. People simply cannot be shifted as casually as pieces of equipment. In any labour planning program, therefore, we are compelled to consider labour mobility not only in economic terms, but having in mind the fact that those from whom we seek mobility must themselves want it. We cannot easily overcome human inertia, "rootedness" in a particular community, fear of the unknown which even the more readily mobile must suffer to some extent, and the other impediments to mobility.

I need hardly point out that complete mobility is more of a fact in the textbooks than in life, even though we in Canada know from our own experience that there is, in fact, a good deal of mobility at all times. It seems to me that mobility must be encouraged rather than demanded; that there must be the necessary financial incentives to encourage it; that the mobile worker and his family must have assurance not only of reasonably permanent employment, but of the customary amenities of organized community life wherever they go. This we have not yet provided, and we have much to learn from other countries which have sought to increase labour mobility.

I will be so bold as to add to this that greater consideration ought to be given to capital mobility. I do not think I am uttering any heresy when I say that it would be more appropriate to bring jobs to workers rather than workers to jobs, bearing in mind the human as well as the economic implications of all economic activity.

I want to emphasize, as I feel I must, the absolute need for an integrated and comprehensive manpower policy if labour planning is to have any meaning at all. It is not enough to have bits and pieces of manpower programs, if they are not co-ordinated and if they come into being merely as stop-gap measures. There must be an over-all perspective of what is going on and what needs to be done. There must be unity of action, regardless of how many divisions there are within the program itself. In short, it is simply not good enough to be able to point to four, or five, or six, or more kinds of programs, each one having to do with manpower, if they do not mesh together.

I can only conclude by saying that labour planning, which is another way of describing manpower policies, can be significant only if it truly is based on and forms an integral part of economic planning generally. One is the indispensable prerequisite of the other.

IV. NEW AREAS OF CO-OPERATION

Agriculture

LAUREN SOTH*

CANADA AND THE UNITED STATES share a common problem with their agricultural industries—the problem of over-production. Our farm output tends to grow faster than the commercial demand from domestic consumers and foreign buyers. At the same time our two countries share a related problem—the problem of hunger in the underdeveloped countries of the world. In these areas, the food supply is not increasing as rapidly as the population. World peace and stability and our own security depend on finding ways to use our immense resources and our technical knowledge to close the widening world food gap.

These issues of surplus and scarcity challenge our inventiveness. Surely this is a field of planning where Canadians and Americans could profitably work together much more than they do. A good beginning for both countries

*Editor of the Editorial Pages, *Des Moines Register & Tribune,* Des Moines, Iowa.

would be to acknowledge that the large problems of food and agriculture cannot be solved by leaving them to the so-called free market.

In advanced industrial economies such as ours, agriculture's market bargaining power is weak. There is inexorable pressure on the individual farmer to increase output regardless of price levels, because by himself he cannot influence total output or total marketings. Large public investment in agricultural research and technical assistance primes the pump of production. The gains from governmental investment in new farm technology are large, but they are largely transmitted to the consuming public in lower prices. Without government programs to restrain output, regulate marketings, and protect prices, farmers would suffer severe losses in income as a consequence of their own productivity. The inelastic demand for food in a rich society means that a large supply sells for less money to the farmer than a small supply.

Thus every advanced industrial nation has found it necessary to intervene in the farm economy. Canada has its Wheat Board and deficiency payments. It has paid direct subsidies on acreage of wheat. The United States has its acreage restriction programs, price supports, and payments to farmers for land idling. Lately the United States has been moving more toward the deficiency payment method, allowing market price supports to fall to a level nearer world export prices.

Canadians frequently have criticized the Americans for their policy of high wheat price supports and sales in world trade at cut-rate prices, charging that this interferes with their normal commercial markets. However, the limitation of wheat production in the United States and the insulation of massive stockpiles from the world market undoubtedly have helped support world and Canadian prices. Let me say, also, that Canada's more practical attitude on sales of grain to China and Russia has helped American wheat growers by relieving our joint surplus. Under the new American policy of low price support and deficiency payments, subsidized commercial wheat exports should be eliminated or at least moderated as a source of irritation between us.

Obviously, the methods used to protect farmers' incomes have a great deal to do with international trade in farm products nowadays, perhaps even more than tariff levels. Should we not, therefore, seek ways of consulting one another more frequently on domestic farm policy and of planning domestic farm programs together? Agriculture Secretary Freeman already has offered to negotiate with the Common Market on domestic farm price supports as well as on tariffs and trade quotas. But in this North American community of two similar agricultural economies, it is even more rational to try to mesh our plans for agriculture.

I suggest that Canada and the United States establish a joint agricultural planning board, to include non-official members from both countries and perhaps ex-officio representatives of their departments of agriculture. This board might make studies and prepare recommendations for Congress and Parliament. If nothing occurred but a constant interchange of plans and ideas, it would be constructive.

Our most pressing question at this stage in history is how we can best use our capacity for food production to show others how to produce food. The Food for Peace Program ought to be an Atlantic Community Food for Peace Program—or at least a North American Food for Peace Program.

The time is overdue for us to face the fact that a non-commercial market exists in the world. This market, which is not really a market, must be supplied if revolution is to be prevented. We must steer our scientific farming resources into these lands to enable them to build up their farming industries. In the interim, we must use our own production surpluses to feed them. This does not destroy commercial markets; in fact, quite the opposite result can be shown. As countries become better fed they become better customers, not just for industrial goods but for farm products as well.

There is only one place to start economic development in a country made up of 70 per cent farmers—and that place is in farming. Canada and the United States together have resources unmatched elsewhere for spurring agricultural development. In this field, more than any other, we have a tremendous advantage over our competitors, China and Russia. I suggest that we maximize this advantage by closer planning of a joint effort.

Energy

ROY A. MATTHEWS*

AMONG THE MANY INTERESTING PROPOSITIONS contained in the Merchant-Heeney *Report* was one concerning the benefits that might accrue from "closer co-operation and co-ordination between our two countries in the production

*Canadian Director of Research, The Canadian-American Committee, Private Planning Association of Canada, Montreal, Quebec. The views expressed here reflect the personal opinions of Mr. Matthews and not those of the Canadian-American Committee.

and distribution of energy, especially electrical energy." The authors of the *Report* suggested that "under appropriate conditions, joint planning and development of resources to that end in various regions would appear to afford promising opportunities," and they recommended "early and serious study of such possibilities."[1]

This is not the first time that the idea of a joint Canadian-American approach to the question of energy development on this continent has been put forward. Such a conception has been discussed by businessmen and government officials many times in the past, but I do not believe it has ever been placed before the public in the way that occurred with the appearance of the Merchant-Heeney *Report*. It may be, therefore, that the issues involved will be subjected to fairly widespread debate over the next few years.

Merchant and Heeney make special mention of electric power, so let us consider that form of energy first. Since Canadian policy on power exports was changed in the late 1950's, we have steadily increased our trade in electricity, and there is every indication that we will continue to do.

There may be opportunities for further developments of the Peace River and Churchill (Hamilton) Falls type, which are essentially export-oriented, although such exploitation of vast but remote hydro resources looks less interesting now that nuclear power is becoming increasingly competitive. Schemes of this kind, with the heavy fixed cost involved in the immensely long transmission lines, must be operated on an essentially round-the-clock basis to be economically efficient, and they are, therefore, in direct competition with nuclear or other thermal facilities. The more conventional hydro installations, on the other hand, located fairly close to civilization and

[1]*Canada and the United States: Principles for Partnership* (Ottawa, 1965), 39.

having low fixed cost, can often be most efficiently utilized for the provision of peaking power—the few hours a day of maximum demand—and thus tend to be complementary to nuclear stations. Consequently it is not too hard to visualize a system under which Canadian power authorities would purchase blocks of cheap American power produced in very large nuclear installations (possibly located on both coasts and operated in conjunction with sea-water desalination plants—a very popular idea in the eastern states and California). In turn the American authorities would buy Canadian hydro-produced peaking power for their heavy load periods.

From this development one can readily envisage an eventual coast-to-coast interlocking of power grids south of the border and perhaps north of it as well, although a duplicate Canadian system would not be strictly necessary in technical or economic terms. With all the power authorities in North America hooked into one huge continental network, electricity could be directed to the place where it was most needed from the point where it could best be obtained. This series of relatively easy steps seems to lead us readily to a continental set-up.

However, while this might represent closer co-operation between the two countries in the power field, it a very long way from being a "joint policy," in any meaningful sense of the term. The situation of a series of interlinked systems is no more than exists now in certain areas of the United States and Canada, and it by no means ensures co-ordinated planning or rational use of the resources involved. One has only to look at the administrative jungle of electric power agencies and authorities in the United States, and recall the bitter and long-standing disputes between private and public power, to recognize that there is a great difference between the pragmatic movement towards continental integration that I have described, and the establishment of a North American energy policy such as is implied by the Merchant-Heeney *Report*. The further stage to joint planning would be the hardest of all to arrange. Nevertheless, I think it could be done and that we should start studying the possibility right away.

If the obstacles to the evolution of a joint policy for the development of the continent's electric power resources appear considerable, they are nothing compared with the difficulties in the way of any such design for the petroleum industry. As is well known, a high proportion of the oil (and its derivatives) produced, processed, and distributed in North America comes from very large international companies with global interests. For such firms a purely continental approach would have little or no appeal, as they are accustomed to moving their supplies around the world as economics and corporate interests dictate. It is a measure of the type of situation created by the international flavour of the oil business that Canada's main producing centre in the continental heartland has found its most logical markets in the western and middle-western provinces and states, while the demands of the eastern provinces have been filled from overseas—mainly Venezuelan—supplies.

Of course, the freedom of the international companies has not been absolute. They have, indeed, been subjected to a wide variety of regulations and restrictions designed to satisfy everyone from the so-called "independent" oil companies to the oil-producing states and provinces and even the Texas Railroad Commission. But this diminution of the international aspect of the oil industry hardly works in the direction of continentalism. Rather it superimposes a regional and vested-interest complication that only further increases the problems. Given this maze of difficulties, one may wonder whether a Canadian-American joint planning arrangement in oil could amount to much more, under present conditions, than an increased

degree of liaison between federal agencies, such as the
National Energy Board and the United States Department
of the Interior.

Electric power and oil represent, respectively, the most
and the least promising prospects for a joint Canadian-
American policy. The remaining energy forms range between these two extremes. Natural gas is perhaps an
obvious candidate for a continental approach because,
unlike oil, it is not, at least up to now, very readily
transported across the oceans. In addition, the natural gas
industry is of more recent foundation and growth than
the oil business and has not had as long to develop com-
plexities of administration and regulation. Gas now crosses
the border in both directions and in large amounts, flowing southward from the Canadian prairies to the American
west and middle-west, and northwards from the northeastern states into Ontario and Quebec. Why not consoli-
date this trade into a joint policy?

It could be done, although there are formidable difficulties. The natural gas industry is, after all, an arm of
the oil industry, and it might be very hard to achieve
joint planing in one without the other. Even if it were
possible to separate the two, and proceed with a common
policy for natural gas, producers of gas would, for the
most part, retain the backing of the oil industry's powerful influence in Washington. This would favour the case
if the balance of forces in the United States supported
continental integration, but would be a considerable
obstacle if no such clear-cut preference were found to
exist. On the Canadian side, I suspect we would encounter
opposition from nationalists and conservationists who
would question the wisdom of allowing the export, under
a policy shaped in part by foreigners, of a non-renewable
resource (as opposed to the power developed from such a
resource in the case of hydro-electricity).

The application of the principle of joint planning to the coal industry raises considerations of a very different kind. To put the matter in its baldest terms, coal mining in Nova Scotia would be virtually destroyed if the system of tariffs and, more important, transport subventions, which enable the Maritimes' product to compete with Pennsylvania coal in central Canada, were withdrawn. The western Canadian coal industry would fare somewhat better because it is insulated by distance from the major producing areas of the United States, but it is small by comparison with the Nova Scotia mines.

From a strictly economic point of view, therefore, continental rationalization of coal production and distribution is eminently logical. However, the social and political problems associated with the present low living standards of the Atlantic Provinces are familiar in Canada, and the prospect of an abandonment, or at least a substantial curtailment, of the coal mining industry would doubtless give rise to fierce reactions. It would seem, therefore, that a move in this direction would be extremely hard to achieve politically, and would stand a chance of success only if it were made part and parcel of a massive program of assistance to Nova Scotia, if not to the entire Atlantic area.

The United States and Canada have adopted completely different policies on the development of nuclear reactors, the United States basing its program on enriched uranium, in which product it has, at present, a world monopoly, while Canada is tying its fortunes to natural uranium. Each country is endeavouring to sell its reactor system to other nations, knowing that such sales will inevitably be followed by continuing orders for the respective fuels.

While a defeat in this fierce, though friendly, battle would not be the end of the uranium business for either country, it would greatly affect trade in this commodity, and one can therefore hardly contemplate any joint arrangements involving the two contestants until the war between the rival systems is over and one or the other becomes dominant.

In conclusion, the outlook for a Canadian-American policy for the development of the continent's energy resources appears mixed, with electric power the most promising case, natural gas and coal seeming somewhat less hopeful, oil a very difficult area indeed, and uranium for the moment out of the running.

I would add only one extra word. Some people might suggest that the proper way to consider a continental energy policy is by looking at the whole energy picture, being prepared to trade off difficulties and disadvantages in one sector against merits and opportunities in others. Indeed, it is possible that the two governments might one day come to look at the matter in this light, but it is not easy to see how the change to such an approach would yield anything more than an averaging of the potential achievements—that is, rather more on oil, say, but somewhat less on electric power.

I suspect a more significant gain could be realized only under circumstances where there existed an underlying political will on the part of the two governments to create a community in energy as a component in some wider vision for our two countries. By way of stretching your imaginations with a bit of fantasy, I would like to conjure up before you the notion of a dedicated group of "North Americans"—like post-war western Europe's "Europeans" —who might see energy as a key to industrial strength, and thus urge the continental integration of the one as tending to produce conditions leading to a similar integration of the other. A supranational authority for energy could appear to such people as a rough North American equivalent of the European Coal and Steel Community, which was an early step in the long series of attempts—some successful, some not—at regional arrangements which culminated in the formation of the Common Market. It is an intriguing thought!

Water

SPERRY LEA*

PROBABLY THE MOST NOTABLE EXAMPLE of Canadian-American planning lies in our so-called "boundary waters," the rivers and lakes existing along our frontiers. Through the International Joint Commission, we have since 1909 worked together to improve the benefits and frustrate the ill effects of these waters on us—or our ill effects on them. Among many past accomplishments, the largest are the St. Lawrence Seaway and the Columbia River Agreement. Much unfinished business remains. Of the present work of the IJC, the most important is exploring ways to ease the double-headed threat to the Great Lakes: fluctuations in their levels and flows—now near record lows—and pollution.

*American Director of Research, The Canadian-American Committee, National Planning Association, Washington, D.C. This paper reflects Mr. Lea's personal views and not those of the Canadian-American Committee.

We could profitably discuss Canadian-American planning in terms of joint steps to improve the quality and manipulate the quantity of water in the Detroit River, to mention just one area of unfinished business along our boundary. But instead, let us explore new dimensions in joint water-planning concepts which reach beyond the traditional scope of our boundary waters to the idea of bringing unused fresh water from remote northern watersheds—mainly Canadian—to places on our continent where this water is needed, or is said to be needed.

Two specific illustrations have appeared: the North American Water and Power Alliance Plan and the Kierans Plan.

Behind the NAWAPA concept is the idea that many problems of water quantity in Canada and the United States might be handled better on a continental basis than by a series of separate regional projects. The plan as presently drawn illustrates one way by which some of the excess run-off from the northwestern region of North America might be redistributed to needy areas of the continent by methods which are technically and economically feasible.

The main collection reservoir for NAWAPA would sprawl at an altitude of 2,000 feet over the Yukon, eastern Alaska, and the northern tip of British Columbia. From a long distribution reservoir in the Canadian Rockies, the Rocky Mountain Trench, the main north-south trunk would convey water through a series of tunnels, lifts and man-made channels to eight states in the arid southwest. Here it would be used mainly for irrigation. Some water would continue on to Mexico. A second, east-west branch of NAWAPA would bring water across the Canadian Prairies through navigable canals to Hudson Bay and the Great Lakes. Independent elements would supply additional water to the Great Lakes from Ontario and

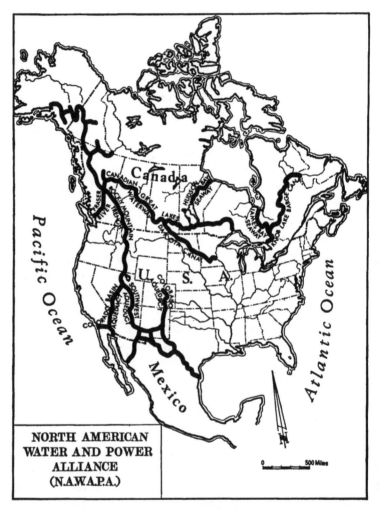

NORTH AMERICAN
WATER AND POWER
ALLIANCE
(N.A.W.A.P.A.)

Quebec. While the main purpose of the system would be to provide water, it would also yield a net output of electric power and extend navigation. The cost of the full plan is estimated at $100 billion and it would take thirty years to build.

The Grand Canal Proposal (Kierans Plan) focuses primarily on the Great Lakes and their adjacent region. Its

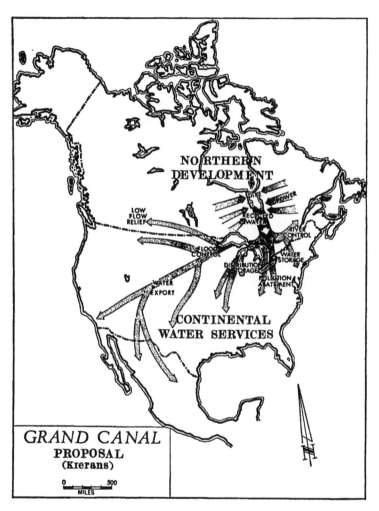

GRAND CANAL
PROPOSAL
(Kierans)

0 ___ 500
MILES

underlying concept is that the full range of problems on the Lakes can best be solved by being able to add—and, just as important, to withdraw—water as conditions demand. The concept also envisages the possibility of using the Great Lakes as a giant distribution manifold for supplying additional water to much of the United States.

In this case the collection reservoir would be an artificial fresh water lake at sea level formed by diking off the southern tip of James Bay, which would then be filled by the outflow of several north-flowing Quebec rivers. This water would be lifted by pumps southward up the Harricanaw River and then flow down the upper Ottawa and the French River to begin a second life in Lake Huron. An alternative all-Canadian route would carry the water from the James Bay area down the Ottawa River to the St. Lawrence above Montreal. An important feature of the Kierans Plan is withdrawing the river water at its usual point of entry into the sea rather than upstream. Thus "recycling" rather than "diversion" is the better word to describe what would happen.

Moving from the outline of these schemes to their implications for joint planning, let us note first that the idea of meeting US water deficiencies with Canadian water is very new. The major American study, *Water Supply, Economics, Technology, and Policy*,[1] notes many possible ways of bringing new water to deficient regions—including by tanker ship—but says not one word about importing Canadian water. The massive study *Resources in America's Future: Patterns of Requirements and Availabilities, 1960–2000*, has two chapters on the water situation in the United States. It discusses a number of Canadian resources 1960–2000,[2] has two chapters on the water situation in the in relation to American needs—from chromium to zinc—but there is no mention of Canadian water resources in relation to the requirements of the United States. It is safe to say that the concept of Canadian water for shared use, or for the more exclusive use of the States did not emerge until the NAWAPA and Kierans Plans were made public in 1964.

---

[1]Hirshleifer, De Haven, and Millman (Chicago, 1960).
[2]H. H. Landsberg, L. L. Fischman, and J. L. Fisher (Baltimore, 1963).

We are confronted, therefore, with an unusual situation in which an idea involving many technicalities has reached the status of a major conversation piece in Canadian-American relations before it has been studied by the experts. This situation offers both advantages and disadvantages. On the one hand, no conventional wisdom tethers us to traditional, and often obsolescent, concepts; and there is an appeal in ideas that are fresh as well as big. On the other, starting from scratch means that the basic facts are insufficiently developed and discussion is confused—perhaps dangerously—by assertions passing for conclusions.

The question of Canadian water for US use is not only too new to be discussed knowledgeably, it is by nature difficult to consider rationally. Those endowed with ample water resources instinctively oppose giving up even small amounts. Americans and their political leaders demonstrate this reflex as vividly as Canadians.

The controversy turns around differing Canadian reactions to the question "Should Canada sell some of its fresh water to the United States?" The answers range from a resounding "no" to a cautious interest in the scheme. But this question is not productive because it is premature. The starting point for a sensible Canadian-American approach to the possible new dimension in water planning is therefore to ask better questions.

We should first test the validity of the proposition that it makes sense to consider Canadian water in relation to American needs. This would require affirmative answers to the following questions:

Do water shortages in fact exist or threaten in the United States?

If so, does the solution require, besides a more efficient use of available water, additional supplies?

If so, considering technical and economic feasibility,

would water from Canada be a logical—or the logical—source of additional supply?

If so, would there be available some Canadian water in excess of foreseeable need in their respective basins?

Reaching adequate answers to these questions would take considerable time. And although the inquiry would, by and large, be carried on in one or the other country, there are essential elements that must be co-ordinated, especially on the third question. While these first questions are being asked, both countries should try to postpone not merely premature verdicts but also commitments to any national solutions to water problems which would be totally incompatible with what might prove to be more rational solutions involving both countries.

If, following research on the first series of questions, the concept of Canadian water for continental needs can be established as a conclusion rather than an assertion, more detailed research—this time undertaken jointly—should be aimed at specific proposals, such as NAWAPA and the Kierans Plan. The particular plans would be probed for crucial defects, the question always being asked whether there is some simpler way of accomplishing the same result. This would require an assessment of the non-economic implications. If it appeared that the broad outlines of a plan were sound, then a range of technical studies would be necessary to determine the optimum choreography of water in the system.

Finally, thought would have to be given to how so vast a public works program could be organized, financed, and managed in two sovereign countries and, where water is concerned, several sovereign provinces, keeping in mind our basically private economies. For the efforts to bring the new dimension to water in North America and to operate the complex hydraulic system in an acceptable way would require to an unprecedented degree official and private planning.

V. AUTOMATION

A Perspective

HUME WRIGHT*

PERSPECTIVE is perhaps the most fundamental of the present needs pertaining to automation in any context, including North American planning. Perspective is needed to dispel serious misapprehensions conjured up by automation and other technological change. It is needed to perceive the importance of the relationship between technological advances and the achievement of such basic and familiar economic and social goals as full employment, a high rate of economic growth, reasonable stability of prices, a viable balance of payments, and an equitable distribution of rising incomes. Perspective is also needed to appreciate fully the social and economic value of adequate measures which facilitate adjustment to technological change. Finally, perspective is required to search out the relevant, to spot the purely speculative, and to apply the test of reasonableness in a vast field of inquiry where extremism flourishes and knowledge is still very inadequate. As Mr. Willard Wirtz, the United States Secretary

*Secretary of the Committee on Economic Growth and Problems of Adjustment, Economic Council of Canada, Ottawa.

of Labour, pointed out in an official report, "At present only limited information is available regarding such basic matters as the extent, rate of introduction, and employment effects of technological developments."[1]

Major studies now underway should certainly improve the position. The United States National Commission on Technology, Automation, and Economic Progress will be presenting its report in 1966, and Harvard University is spending ten years and $5 million—made available by IBM—on its Program on Technology and Society.

Automation, narrowly defined, can be described as the regulation of the process of production by mechanical, electronic, and other self-operating devices. This definition covers the concept of "feedback" or closed-loop control which is often illustrated by citing the regulation of a household heating system by an ordinary thermostat. However, the word automation is generally used so broadly that it conveys much the same meaning as technological change, which includes automation no matter how either term is defined. Technological change can be defined comprehensively as any change in material, equipment, methods, organization, or product which alters the quantity or quality of labour required per unit of physical output.

To assess present needs pertaining to technological change, it is first necessary to appreciate generally, and without misapprehensions, how technological advances relate to a high rate of growth and other basic economic and social goals.

The rate of economic growth depends basically on the pace of productivity gains and increases in employment. Productivity growth is a blend of numerous ingredients some of which are rather elusive. In its *First Annual Review* the Economic Council of Canada lists six basic

groups of factors which contribute importantly to productivity gains:
- "increased investment in human resources to improve knowledge and skills,
- improved mobility of resources so that they can move easily and smoothly towards their most efficient employment,
- greater specialization and better organization of production,
- swifter and more effective technological advances,
- enlarged investment in fixed capital, and
- more initiative and enterprise in exploring new and better ways to use economic resources more productively, under the spur of competition and the lure of higher returns."

It is, therefore, the combination of all such factors, including technological change, which results in the growth of productivity. The combined influence of all of them can be measured in terms of output per person employed—a convenient measure of productivity which is adhered to in this text. But no matter how it is measured, the key point about productivity is that it is the prime source of improvements in average real income per capita —in other words, average living standards. "Moreover," according to the Economic Council's *Review*, "without adequate productivity growth, an industrial nation's competitive position and its international payments position may be subjected to disturbing pressures and strains." The Council also states that, ". . . high rates of productivity growth must be achieved if the goal of sustained high-employment is to be reached and maintained. . . . It is this combination of sustained high-employment and sustained advances in productivity which together provide the basis for sustained economic growth."

The Canadian experience since the war shows rather

strikingly that substantial advances in productivity and high levels of employment have gone together and vice versa. In the first decade of the post-war period, productivity increased by an average of 3.2 per cent a year. During this same period employment was at high levels with the unemployment rate averaging 3.2 per cent. In contrast, from 1956 to 1965 productivity increases sank to an average annual rate of 1 per cent while unemployment averaged 6 per cent.

By definition, any gains whatsoever in productivity, that is, output per person employed, inexorably reduce the number of persons required to produce a given quantity of goods and services. This relationship is sometimes used to make estimates, which can lead to serious misapprehensions, about hypothetical reductions in employment caused by productivity growth which, for this purpose, goes under the name of automation. In this way, it quite often is alleged that automation is reducing employment by some 3,000 jobs a week. The basis for this sort of allegation can best be explained in specific terms. Let us assume, for example, that employment in 1965, in Canada, approached 7 million with a 2.4 per cent growth in productivity, which is the average annual rate incorporated in the Economic Council targets for the period from 1963 to 1970. Using these figures, it can be said, although it makes a curious statement, that this year's output could be produced next year with some 160,000 fewer workers. This figure is then reduced to a weekly basis and used to make the familiar allegations.

In reality, this kind of figuring provides no basis whatsoever for alarm either about automation or employment. In the first place, the estimates are based on the wholly unwarranted assumption that total output will stop growing. In fact, in Canada, it has more than doubled since the war. Secondly, the estimates are based not on the employment impact of automation but on hypothetical effects of productivity growth, which, of course, reflect factors other than automation. As a matter of fact, the same allegations could have been made long before automation was ever heard of. Altogether, these estimates are nothing more than an irrelevant statistical restatement of the obvious; namely, that increases in productivity reduce the number of persons required to do a given amount of work.

To take a dim view of automation generally, on the grounds that it reduces the number of people needed to do a certain amount of work, would be to misconstrue the essence of productivity growth. On these grounds it would, in fact, be equally logical to take a dim view of many other factors including education, better health standards, better industrial relations and research and development, which also improve productivity and growth capacity.

The utilization of growing capacity is a crucial matter which relates mainly to the demand side of the economy. An appropriate demand and supply relationship of vital importance is sustaining growth in employment and output as part of the attainment of basic goals.

The broad dimensions of past economic growth are known and this knowledge provides additional perspective in assessing the implications of technological change. In Canada, for example, total real output approximately doubled from 1946 to the beginning of 1964 while at the same time productivity rose by close to 50 per cent. These developments took place along with a net increase of over 1.6 million new jobs and a 30 per cent increase in living standards as measured by real output per capita. And, in the immediate past, output and employment have surged. From the middle of 1964 to the middle of 1965, employment increased by 276,000 more jobs and some pronounced manpower shortages cropped up, although unemployment, while much reduced, was still too high in some parts of the country—but not in parts, it should be noted, which are associated with the rapid diffusion of new technology.

Altogether, the evidence indicates clearly that it is a misconception to look on technological change, including automation, as an enemy of high employment. On the contrary, it is plainly evident that technological advances contribute to high rates of productivity growth which have gone hand in hand with high levels of employment. This alliance of high employment and vigorous productivity growth, underpinned by requisite demand, is exactly what is required for the attainment of major economic and social goals.

In this perspective there can be no doubt about the importance and logic of fully adequate measures to facilitate adjustments to technological change. Efficient adjustment procedures contribute to gains in productivity growth and so advance the attainment of basic goals. Conversely, this attainment is obstructed by failure to facilitate change. As the Economic Council states in its *First Annual Review*:

> When sudden, severe and inequitable burdens—both economic and social—fall on individual workers and firms, and on particular communities, it is natural to expect strong pressures aimed at slowing down, or even halting, the processes of change. Governments are urged and tempted to subsidize and support declining and relatively less efficient industries. Employers are tempted to seek increased shelter behind trade restrictions or in the form of restrictive trade practices. Labour unions are tempted to exert strong pressures to cling to old working rules. Obviously, if such defensive and negative approaches prevail, both change and growth will be curtailed.

However, in recent years, the Council points out, ". . . increasing attention has been given to an alternative approach to the problems created by rapid change—that of facilitating adjustment from declining to expanding activities, and of increasing the mobility and adaptability of resources in the interests of maximizing both their efficient use and their incomes."

Such increased mobility of resources, especially manpower resources, clearly requires interrelated and complementary public and private action with respect to basic education, training, retraining, and all aspects of mobility including job placement. It also poses the need for the application of new approaches in the field of labour-management co-operation, including advance notice of changes, the curtailment of recruitment to minimize displacement, and the transfer of displaced employees to other in-company jobs, in-company training and so on.

Involved also is an overriding requirement which amounts almost to a prerequisite for fully effective action to facilitate manpower changes. This is the need to develop, present, and forward manpower information on a specific enough basis to be used to good effect in dealing with the current requirements of the manpower situation and its anticipated future development. Some far-flung companies, for example, are programming detailed personnel information for computer use. Then, when a specific job opening comes up, no suitable candidate already with the company need be overlooked on "out of sight, out of mind" grounds. So applied, the computer, it should perhaps be observed, represents an extraordinarily efficient filing system and not the incarnation of "Big Brother."

Procedures of this sort clearly facilitate the operation within a company of what might be called an effective internal labour market which helps to get round pegs into round holes and generally makes needed adjustments and the best use of human resources. These internal company labour markets operate in the context of the general employment market. This, it is widely agreed, is an imperfect market. Indeed, the service and facilities offered by

the employment market do not compare with those provided by other free markets such as, for example, suburban
supermarkets, securities markets or the automobile market.
In these complex and dynamic public markets great and
effective efforts are made to facilitate the matching up of
supply and demand as expeditiously and accurately as
possible. In contrast, the general employment market
appears to be an outmoded and make-shift affair, which
operates in a willy-nilly sort of way, mainly perhaps on
hearsay, even though its function is to serve the manpower
needs of the nation as well as to fill a need which for most
individuals could hardly be more basic, namely, to earn
a living. Measures are now being taken towards strengthening this market which will be called upon to help match
up individuals with the 1.5 million additional jobs needed
in Canada in the 1963–70 period, as well as to facilitate an
immense number of other individual adjustments arising
out of growth and change.

It appears entirely possible that fears of automation,
along with the human and economic costs associated with
them, would recede rapidly with the operation of a
modernized employment market underpinned with suitable training and appropriate general demand. Even then,
however, the fulfilment of present needs might to some
extent be bedevilled by fears of the ultimate consequences
of automation.

These fears for the future appear to be an inherent
aspect of the present implications of automation. For in an
era of space exploration, nuclear fission, and advances in
the development of something akin to artificial intelligence
it does not take great imagination to conceive of the possibility that ultimately a small fraction of the population
might be able to produce an abundance of goods and
services for all. This might require work for pay and
money, as it now functions, to go out of style. In the face
of such ultimate possibilities, there does not seem to be

much of great relevance that can be gleaned from going back into the history of automation. It seems largely irrelevant to recall that, for example, in the eighteenth century James Watt used a closed-loop system to control the speed of his steam engine; or that in 1806 the French engineer Jacquard used punch cards in developing a completely automatic loom for weaving patterns of cloth; or that Charles Babbage, the father of the modern computer, was born at the time of the French Revolution. Nor does it seem particularly relevant to recollect that in the past men have often feared machines and have sometimes, like the Luddites in nineteenth-century England, destroyed them.

What is now entirely relevant is that policies which could ultimately be appropriate are not only irrational in terms of present needs but that undue preoccupation with them can act as a drag on advances required now. In relation to present needs, the development of a tendency to resist technological change for fear of unknown eventualities can almost be likened to a tendency to put on the brakes when driving up a long and steep hill for fear of what is over the other side. Hopefully, any such tendency will be alleviated by good sense and studies, like the Harvard Program, of the required depth, breadth, and competence.

For the visible future as for the present and certainly for the Canadian part of North America, the conclusion is unmistakable and inescapable. The prime need is for more, not less, automation; although, like electricity, its widespread use to power economic growth and higher living standards necessitates fully adequate measures to protect individuals from its potential dangers. Everything centres around the purpose of making better use of human and other resources so as to better satisfy human wants. This, I take it, is also the central purpose of North American planning.

Employment

GEORGE BURT*

THE WORD "AUTOMATION" is barely adequate today to describe the technological revolution in which we are involved. More and more, words and phrases such as "cybernation" (meaning automation based on the use of computers), "the new technology," and "the scientific revolution" are called into use to refer to the intense efforts being put into scientific research and engineering development. Never has as much money and creativity been concentrated on the deliberate planning of technological breakthroughs as in the post-war period. It has been estimated that of all the scientists who have ever been born since the beginning of human history, 90 per cent are alive and at work today. And the majority of the present generation is engaged in preparing for the introduction of the future's discoveries in technology.

Our concern is with the consequences of a rapidly increasing rate of technological advance, rather than its physical application. I propose therefore to use the word "automation" in its broad sense as shorthand for the lengthier phrases mentioned. Our concern is with the impact of automation on jobs and incomes, prices, and our potential for remedying the many unresolved defects

*Canadian Director, Canadian Region, United Auto Workers, Windsor, Ontario.

of our economy and society—poverty, unemployment, unsatisfactory economic growth, and a lengthy catalogue of unmet public needs.

Let me say at once that the assertion that automation creates more jobs than it destroys is false and completely contradictory. The whole impulse to automate a process is to save enough on labour, blue- or white-collar, to pay the cost of the new machinery or electronic equipment and show a profit on the investment. There would be no incentive to automate if the amount of labour saved by the equipment were not many times greater than the amount of labour required to produce it.

It is not only manual, unskilled labour that may be displaced. In the automobile and aerospace industries, whose several hundred thousand employees the United Auto Workers represents, a process is now in use called photogrammetry. A clay mock-up of a complex part is photographed in three dimensions; the pictures are automatically translated into a code for punch tape; and the tape is fed through machines that do the work formerly performed by diemakers, template makers, and draftsmen—all highly skilled classifications.

Even more astonishing and "thought-saving" as well as labour-saving is the IBM-designed machine in use at General Motors called DAC-1 (Design Augmented by Computers), which carries the process right back to the auto stylist and designer. It ties together a computer, a television picture tube, and a microfilm machine. Line drawings of automobile components are flashed on the picture tube from data fed into the computer. The operator can enlarge or redraw the design or rotate it to a different perspective and the machine will "remember" each change in the drawing. Within thirty seconds, microfilmed copies of the revised drawings can be produced and then enlarged into working drawings. The machine can also produce electronic tapes which can be fed into drafting machines that will automatically produce finished engineering drawings.

Finally, it is possible to feed additional engineering problems into the computer, and, if the designer using it stops to think, the computer will spend any available free time, down to a thousandth of a second, working on another problem.

The potentialities of the machine for replacing some of the highest skilled workers in the auto industries, and in the other metal industries, are obvious. In industry after industry, the computer may take over the jobs, not only of skilled and semi-skilled blue-collar workers, but of clerical workers and some in executive positions.

As we enter a period of accelerating application of automation, we are also facing the population explosion of the second half of this century. Thus we are challenged on two counts. The dual challenges of automation and population growth present us with staggering problems. Jobs in increasing numbers—each year, each month, each week —must be created to provide employment to millions of people entering the labour market in the next decade, if we are not to face mounting unemployment.

One of the responses to these challenges that must be prepared, I suggest, is a redefinition of what we mean by "full employment." In its *First Annual Review*, the Economic Council of Canada forecasts that "we require a net increase of 1.5 million jobs from 1963 to 1970." Achievement of that goal is essential if unemployment is to be held down to a reasonably acceptable minimum level. Success will require sustained and adequate economic growth over the long term, which, the Council insists, must rest upon "an appropriate combination of strong expansionary policies to generate adequate levels of demand . . . in support of rapidly expanding employment."

Yet increased demand for goods and services alone will not be enough. From past experience the trade union movement knows that there has been no genuine commitment, on the part of Canadian governments to date, to the "strong expansionary policies" called for by the Council, or to full-employment economic policies. The trade union movement has relied on, and will continue to exploit to the fullest extent, our influence on the private economy through collective bargaining as long as governments decline to fill their full role in achieving such desirable and essential goals.

The trade union movement, and the UAW with special vigor, I think I may assert, has fought for a fair share of the fruits of rising productivity. Increasingly, from contract to contract, we are taking our share in the form of new opportunities for leisure or paid time off the job. There is no doubt that we are going to confirm that trend in future negotiations. We have reduced the work week, increased the number of paid holidays, lengthened vacations, created or acknowledged new reasons or excuses for absence from work, such as paid leaves for study and bereavement pay for absence to attend to funeral arrangements. As industry and the state have raised the school-leaving age, we have been negotiating successfully to reduce retirement age. Recently, longer relief and rest periods and coffee breaks have become increasingly common in both plants and offices.

The Economic Council's *Review* has called for a 5 per cent rate of growth annually, and our economy is capable of achieving it if we make full use of our manpower resources and automation. Significant increases in our standard of living will be realized if that rate of growth is achieved. Personal income after taxes will rise sharply, and in the last quarter of this century, could well exceed the amount required to purchase the generally accepted basic needs of the day. It is unlikely, however, that work-ing time would not be drastically reduced before that high level of personal income is reached, a development which would not necessarily prevent reaching it but might delay doing so. People are likely to prefer more leisure than more goods, as goods become more plentiful and cheap and make less and less of a contribution to the alleviation of drudgery.

If we leave out the factor of increasing leisure, the prospects for the future become nightmarish. But an economist of the year 1900 could easily have reached a similar conclusion about the present by assuming that certain components of the equation would remain fixed. In the year 1900 the typical work-week was 60 hours, yielding a work year of 3,120 hours. An economist of that day could calculate accurately that the Canadian economy in 1964 would provide about 14 billion man-hours of work. He could also foresee accurately the growth of population. He could divide 14 billion man-hours by the 3,120 average hours of work per year characteristic of his day and come up with the conclusion that there would be jobs in the private economy for only 4½ million persons. This would have left 2½ million unemployed, since a labour force of about 7 million was projected for 1964. Such a frightening preview of the mass unemployment of the 1960's may have led him to wonder whether any relationship between work and the income required to purchase a minimum standard of subsistence would exist.

We had serious unemployment in Canada as the 1960's approached, exceeding 700,000 at the bottom of the worst of the post-war recessions. But we did not suffer the stag-gering proportion of unemployed that might have been anticipated. Instead, we bridged a major part of the gap between available hours of work and a greatly enlarged labour force by reducing the work-week and extending paid vacations and paid holidays to sections of the labour force that had never enjoyed them before. As a result, contrary to the economist's assumption about the work-week, hours worked per week averaged close to 40 in 1964, well below the 60 estimated in 1900. In addition, with an average higher school-leaving age and an average lower retirement age, millions who would otherwise have had to be counted as unemployed were not in the labour market.

Full employment today means something quite different from the same expression used in 1900. Then people took for granted a work-day from sun-up to sundown, six or seven days a week, for everyone from age six to age eighty or more. Today full employment means 40 hours or less of work per week for most of those within a much narrower age span and with interruptions of several kinds during the day, the week, and the year. What I am suggesting is that we have kept open the possibility of achieving full employment by redefining it.

The great achievements in science and technology that we are almost certain to apply to our productive capacity in the next twenty years will justify a progressive reduction of the work-day, or the work-week, or both. They will also justify, in the view of the trade union movement, a more equitable sharing of the fruits of economic advance than is now being encouraged by government policies or permitted by the managers of the private economy. These achievements should make possible a vast increase in the production of goods and services to meet the public needs as well as private needs of the people. They should provide the means to build many more schools, hospitals, home and community facilities, to expand our highway and air-port programs, and to deal in an emergency manner with the gigantic pollution and conservation of resources problems that confront us. They should be used to assist us in a successful attack on poverty in this country, to raise the standard of living of all families in the lower- and middle-income brackets, and to enable us to accept our full share of responsibility for assistance to the peoples of the developing nations of the world.

In other words we want to see the savings, achieved from the increased productivity made possible by automation, translated into social capital for investment in education and social services, and not reserved to enhance the wealth and power of large corporations.

Since society as a whole benefits from technological advance, society through governments must accept responsibility for planning and controlling the application of automation.

We in the UAW regard the growing body of scientific and technical knowledge computerized into the work place, the home, and the shops and stores as a national resource. We do little enough at the moment in planning the use of our natural resources; we cannot afford not to plan the use of our scientific knowledge. We must stop "flying blind" into the age of automation, and cease relying on the blind forces of the market-place to give us a sense of direction.

Our choice is not whether the new technologies will be applied or not. Man has always made use of his discoveries, though not always humanely or wisely. Our choice is whether they will be used to wipe out poverty, ignorance, and disease to establish a new measure of material and individual security, or whether they will be used to create new nightmares of dislocation and hostility to change and the future. Our choice is whether we shall find the means to use the abundance made possible by the new technology by sharing it, or whether we shall allow ourselves to be overcome by a glut of gadgetry and luxury unrelated to man's needs. We in the labour movement believe our choice is already made.

VI. TECHNICAL CHANGE

Electric Power

CHARLES F. LUCE*

CHANGES IN TECHNOLOGY often are the result of new needs. My statements will therefore, concern the electric power industry, which offers so many examples of technology responding to new and expanding needs. And they will attempt to relate this new technology to opportunities for joint planning and co-operative ventures between Canada and the United States.

When the first central station systems were built, electric loads were light. Then electricity was generated by small, relatively inefficient plants, each serving its community on an isolated basis. As both population and per capita consumption of electricity increased, total electrical loads grew in geometric proportions. Larger, more efficient generating plants had to be, and were, developed. Transmission technology progressed, too, to cope with these

*Administrator, Bonneville Power Administration, United States Department of the Interior, Portland, Oregon.

changing needs. Previously isolated electric systems became interconnected to share the output of larger, more
economic generating units to take advantage of diversity
in peak loads, to reduce reserve requirements, and the like.

Only twenty-five years ago the largest generators did
not exceed 100,000 kilowatts capacity. The largest transmission line could carry only about 300,000 kilowatts at
287,000 volts, and transmission distance did not exceed
300 miles. Today the electric industry is building single
thermal generators of one million kilowatts capacity, and
transmission lines of 500,000 volts and higher with the
capacity to carry the entire output of such a generator
1,000 miles or more. Even larger generators are appearing
and they need not be located close to load centers.

The first major electric grid on the North American
continent, if not in the world, was developed in Ontario
shortly after the turn of the century, and Ontario Hydro's
pioneering has had a strong influence on the development
of our hydro program in the Pacific Northwest. A significant start toward integrating and co-ordinating electric
systems in the United States was made in the 1920's, and
several jointly-owned generating plants were built in that
period. Co-ordination was stimulated by the Second World
War when it was necessary to pool the existing capacity
of many systems to meet wartime emergency demands
without curtailing service. Today, 97 per cent of the
United States generating capacity is interconnected to
some degree. Interconnections vary from low capacity ties
between two systems for emergency purposes only to
fully integrated pools, such as the Pacific Northwest Power
Pool, to meet the combined needs of the entire interconnected group. The recently completed National Power
Survey, conducted by the Federal Power Commission in
co-operation with all segments of the industry, public and
private, concluded: "Most of the existing networks were
not designed for and are incapable of achieving full

co-ordination, but they represent much technological pioneering and co-operative effort. They are a solid beginning for the stronger interties now being built and planned for the future."

The Survey encourages more and stronger regional interconnections and planning by which all electric utilities, public and private, can plan and build facilities to meet their combined needs to the mutual advantage of themselves and their consumers. Technology is such, the Survey points out, that the opportunity for a fully co-ordinated power supply network is immediate, and not some distant dream. It stresses the numerous benefits of co-ordination and interconnection of which economies of scale, savings through diversity, and reduction of reserve requirements stand out.

The economies of scale are indeed exciting. A one-million-kilowatt coal-burning unit should show savings, according to the Survey, of 20 to 30 per cent in capital costs over a similar 100,000 kilowatt unit. And under base-load operating conditions, the savings, including fuel, should be about 30 to 40 per cent. Comparable advantages of scale are also found in nuclear plants. Only the largest electric systems, by themselves, can finance or utilize the output of such large units. However, through proper co-ordination of systems on an area, regional, or inter-regional basis, these economies can be realized by all systems. The economies of scale in transmission are similarly great. A 500,000-volt transmission line, occupying a right of way not much wider than a 230,000-volt line, can carry four times as much electricity at one-half the unit cost.

By 1980, the Survey predicts, electric utilities can save literally billions of dollars in generating expenses by sharing load diversity through co-ordinated planning and operations. Peak loads vary between regions seasonally, hourly, and at random for such reasons as daily changes in weather. Texas and Arizona, for example, have summer peaks because of air-conditioning and irrigation pumping. The Pacific Northwest has a winter peak largely because of heating requirements. By exchanging power during off-peak seasons, each region can supply part of the peak load of the other. This is the basic rationale behind the Pacific Northwest–Pacific Southwest inter-tie now under construction. There also is important diversity between regions because of time-zone changes. As the sun moves west, lights go on at different times, and east-west exchanges of power can help meet peak loads, thus saving peak-generating requirements of utilities in different time zones. By 1980 the Survey sees a saving of as much as 30 million kilowatts of installed generating capacity through co-ordination by taking advantage of the various kinds of diversity.

Today, in the United States, generating reserves average about 25 per cent of the peak-load requirements of individual systems. Reserves are needed to maintain uninterrupted service during periods of unexpected generator or transmission outages, during scheduled outages for maintenance, and as a margin of safety should loads suddenly grow faster than anticipated. Through co-ordination and interconnection the Survey estimates that, by 1980, average reserves need be only 15 per cent of peak loads—a saving of about 40 per cent in reserve requirements. Reserves of each interconnected system, or each interconnected region, can be utilized to serve the other because the statistical probability of simultaneous outages on two or more systems is infinitesimal.

The same sort of efficiencies—and economies—can be and are being achieved by Canadian utilities at an accelerating pace. But I suggest we need not confine these advantages of co-ordination and interconnection within our respective borders. Additional economies of the same nature can be achieved through broader and stronger inter-connections between systems in our two countries. Canada's population is concentrated just north of the United States border, and Canadian loads typically are closer to American load centres than to other Canadian load centres. The opportunities for co-ordination are enormous. To take advantage of these opportunities requires free trade of electrical energy across our borders.

The new treaty between Canada and the United States for joint development of the Columbia River is an outstanding example. Under the treaty, Canada is building three storage dams on the upper Columbia which will enable downstream American dams to produce, initially, an additional 2.8 million kilowatts of low-cost firm power. Half of this extra power goes to each nation. However, because the present British Columbia market cannot absorb immediately such a huge block of power, Canada decided to sell her share in the States for thirty years. It also is too large a block of power for the Pacific Northwest area of the United States to absorb immediately, so for the period it will be surplus to Northwestern needs it will be sold in the Pacific Southwest, as far as 1,000 miles from the generators. The power will be carried over the intertie lines, without which the treaty probably could not have been implemented.

Already there are six important interconnections between our two countries: the one with Detroit Edison which despite its relative low voltage (115-kv) has, because of the short distance, 600,000 kilowatts of capacity; the 230-kv ties at St. Lawrence Seaway Dam; Niagara Falls; Nelway, British Columbia; and Blaine, Washington—the 500-kv interconnection at Blaine initially being operated at 230-kv.

The three interconnections in the Northwest part of the United States have provided important mutual benefits.

Both the Bonneville Power Administration system and British Columbia Hydro have relied on these interconnections in emergencies. They enable both systems to reduce reserves, and to use the reservoirs of the other. For example, because of surplus water conditions on our system and deficiencies in British Columbia, the Bonneville system today has nearly 200 million kilowatt-hours of energy stored in BC Hydro reservoirs. This is accomplished by our providing BC Hydro excess energy from our system, while BC Hydro holds in its reservoirs water it normally would have to release to meet its own loads. BC Hydro will release the water to produce the energy to return to our system when we need it. These interconnections also permit BC Hydro to sell interruptible power to northwestern industries, and for Bonneville Power Administration and BC Hydro to sell surpluses across the border for steam displacement.

With the economic transmission distance for large blocks of power now 1,000 miles, and with distances of 2,000 miles within reach, development becomes feasible for the large hydro resources in Canada which hitherto have been too remote from load centres. Among these very large potential developments is the proposed Churchill Falls (until recently called Hamilton Falls) project in Labrador. Present proposals contemplate a 4 to 6 million-kilowatt hydro project, with power being marketed in Quebec, New York and possibly New England. An interim report by Manitoba Hydro shows that the hydro potential of the Nelson River Basin exceeds 5 million kilowatts. Power could be marketed on both sides of the border, in Winnipeg, Minneapolis, and St. Paul. At Mica Creek, one of the three treaty storage projects on the upper Columbia, some 2 million kilowatts can be installed. Altogether, the National Power Survey identifies some 7 million kilowatts of Canadian hydroelectric power which could be developed for export to the United States for periods up to twenty-five years—the limit on National Energy Board export licenses—and estimates that 4 million kilowatts will be imported by this country by 1980. Canada likewise has great coal and nuclear resources to fuel steam-fired plants of efficient and economic size from which some of the output could be exported, if it exceeds the immediate requirements of Canadian markets.

This kind of kilowatts-across-the-border planning would be a two-way street. American hydro and steam-generated kilowatts could flow into Canada as economics and joint planning dictate. There appear to be no serious legal problems. The National Energy Board Act of 1959, of course, limits Canadian export licenses to twenty-five years, but this is an adequate period for co-ordination. Further, as reported in the National Power Survey, the Dominion government, in October 1963, announced a policy of encouraging the export of surplus power to the United States and the construction of the necessary inter-connections between Canadian and American power systems. In the United States, the Federal Power Act requires non-federal utilities to obtain Federal Power Commission permits for exports of electrical energy, with a prohibition only against exports which would impair the sufficiency of electric supply within the United States or which would impede, or tend to impede, the co-ordination in the public interest of facilities subject to the jurisdiction of the Commission. Also in the United States an Executive Order requires a Federal Power Commission permit for the construction, operation, maintenance, or connection of facilities at the border which would be used for the transmission of electric energy. In the Pacific Northwest there has been no difficulty obtaining the necessary permits for connections with British Columbia.

Electric loads in both Canada and the United States will continue to grow rapidly in response to the increasing needs of growing populations. In the past seven years, the

United States population increased by 20 million, or nearly 12 per cent. Canada's population growth, though smaller numerically, was at a rate one-third again as fast, or almost 16 per cent. Power requirements in the United States in the next ten years will approximately double, and those of Canada more than double. Within this period our two countries will have to invest as much in new generation, transmission, and distribution facilities as we have in the previous eighty years of the industry. It becomes imperative that each of our nations gets the most for its dollar through international, as well as interregional, power planning, and pooling. Such planning must include large expenditures for research and development—in such matters as direct-current transmission and superconductors, and exotic sources of electric energy—to facilitate interconnections.

Kilowatts-across-the-border planning has several advantages for Canada. Sale to the United States of electric energy production in excess of Canadian needs in the early years would help finance the development of Canadian power potential otherwise not economically feasible at present. In the case of the treaty storage projects, the sale of Canada's share to the United States is financing virtually the entire cost. It will assure Canadians of developed domestic sources of supply for home markets when needed.

For Americans, a free flow of electricity across the border will provide power at load centres at prices competitive with alternative sources in the United States. Canadian hydro available for peaking purposes will enhance the feasibility of large new thermal plants in our country. For both nations it will mean realization of the maximum advantages of scale, of diversity, and reduced reserve requirements, the maximum efficient use of our resources, and, most important of all, lower-cost power for our people.

Metallic Minerals

J. GORDON PARR*

PLANNING, however logically it may be developed, is usually based upon premises that lie outside the control of the planners: the planned education of a child rests upon a congenital mental ability; and the planned economy of a country depends upon the availability of natural resources. In the twentieth century it would be reassuring to think that we had reached a stage of civilization at which we might temper what is good business with an awareness of our good fortune. For Canada is rich in natural mineral wealth. Our greatest single class of exports is that of minerals and the metals derived from them. These represent a total annual value of more than $2 billion—one-third of our total exports.

Table I shows that about one-half of the dollar value of our mineral and metallic exports is in the form of raw material, or material that has been processed only to the point that eases freight costs. Table II shows the distribution of our exports to major consumers: we export, to all countries, about 60 per cent of our total mineral production, of which 60 per cent is taken by the United States. The seemingly high figure of crude mineral exports is

*Dean, Faculty of Applied Science, University of Windsor, Windsor, Ontario. While conversations with my colleagues, and particularly with Dr. W. G. Phillips, may be reflected in parts of this paper, the responsibility for inaccuracies and fallacies is entirely mine.

TABLE I

Importance of Mineral Exports

1963	Billions of dollars	Percentages
Gross national product	43	
Total exports	6.8	16% GNP
Crude mineral exports	1.2	
Processed mineral exports	1.0	
Total mineral exports	2.2	33% exports
Manufactured exports of mineral origin	0.5	7% exports
Total mineral production	3.0	

TABLE II*

Distribution of Mineral Exports

1963	Billions of dollars	Percentages
Total crude and processed mineral exports	2.2	
to United States	1.3	60
to United Kingdom	0.4	18
to Japan	0.1	5

*Data from Mineral Resources Division, Department of Mines and Technical Surveys, Ottawa.

largely contributed by our exports of fuels, uranium oxide, asbestos, and iron ore. I shall deal only with metallic minerals, which either in their raw form, or smelted into metal, represent about $1.3 billion of export trade. And to bring my figures to some sort of focus, I shall take the example of our iron ore exports.

In 1963 we exported to the United States more than $200 million worth of iron ore and concentrate. In round numbers, this represents 10 million tons of iron. Assuming that all the energy and raw materials needed for the mining of the iron ore are Canadian in origin, and that through some cycle, however complex, the $200 million keeps Canadians in work at $3.00 per hour, our iron ore shipments represent about seventy million man-hours of

Canadian work. That is, if all the receipts from our iron ore shipments to the States went into the Canadian purse, thirty-five thousand Canadians were kept occupied.

Iron ore sells at approximately 1 cent per pound of contained iron. If the ore is converted into steel, the steel sells at a little more than 5 cents per pound. That is, had our iron ore exports been converted into steel in Canada, five times as many people would have been employed in Canada, in the exploitation of our iron ore reserves. Going a stage further, and assuming that the steel had been made into cars, refrigerators, and machines—manufactured goods—selling at about $1 a pound, then one hundred times as many men would have been potentially employable by the tonnage of iron ore exported. We might have employed three and a half million men in the production of manufactured goods from the iron ore.

I should like to comment on this familiar and elementary sort of argument which can be applied to many other Canadian raw materials. But first, I would like to point out a technological fact that is not as well appreciated as it should be. It is not through any lack of technical and engineering skill that Canada exports raw material rather than crude or refined metal. Our metal-producing industries are generally well advanced in their methods. The steel industry in Canada is technologically ahead of that in the United States: innovations in our blast-furnace practice and steelmaking processes have preceded acceptance in the States by five or ten years. To be fair, it should also be mentioned that the innovations were rather well researched in Europe and Russia before Canada developed them further. The small size of our industry, and the demand for greater output, have encouraged innovation. But our manufacturing industries are not so well advanced. And the case that I have put in its simplest terms—one which we hear fairly frequently—offers a strong argument for the growth of Canadian manufacture. However, the circumstances are not so simple as they might seem, and the situation I have exemplified with respect to iron ore has several flaws.

First, in bemoaning by implication the fact that the United States takes our raw materials and nourishes its industry with them, we must not forget that we in Canada do the same sort of thing. For example, the annual Canadian aluminum production in the 1960's has been about $30 million—every bit of it from imported ore. Two-thirds of our ingot production is exported—about $5 million worth to the United States for further fabrication into items that we subsequently import. However, the situation is a difficult one to unravel; some of the fabricating plants in the States are owned by the Canadian company, but two-thirds of the stock of the Canadian company is held by Americans.

Second, while the fabrication of ore into fully manufactured goods in Canada would employ additional Canadians, an equivalent number of Americans might be put out of work.

Third, the iron ore properties, and other mineral resources, are not entirely Canadian-owned or operated.

Fourth, the expansion of processing industries and the establishment of manufacturing industries to work the iron ore into finished products implies a capitalization that Canadians might be reluctant to provide.

Fifth, if in the spirit of experiment, we were to establish plants and employ three million immigrants for the production of cars and other commodities from our iron ore, our export market must grow at least proportionately to the increased population. And the sale of cars, and other manufactured goods, is increasingly competitive. The United States can handle a very large product volume, with resulting economies. Japan, through what we like to believe is cheap labour, but more probably because of a more advanced technology, can produce things more economically than we can. The United Kingdom has a large domestic market and concentrated populations nearby (although it would appear that even this advantage is not quite enough).

Before trying to strike some sort of balance between the potential of our mineral wealth and the problems of utilizing it more effectively, I have to offer additional figures.

Let us compare steel production with population in Canada, the United States, the United Kingdom, and Japan (Table III). It should be pointed out that 1958 was a poor year for the United States steel industry. But

TABLE III

Steel Production

	1958			1962		
	Population (millions)	Steel (million tons)	Ratio (steel per person)	Population (millions)	Steel (million tons)	Ratio (steel per person)
Canada	17.1	4.0	0.24	18.6	6.5	0.35
United States	175.0	77.3	0.44	187.0	89.2	0.48
United Kingdom	51.8	19.9	0.39	53.4	20.8	0.39
Japan	91.5	12.1	0.13	94.9	27.5	0.27

Data from *Statistical Yearbook, 1963*, United Nations.

the figures do indicate two facts which, I believe, are relevant. First, steel production per capita in the United States and the United Kingdom is fairly constant, while that of Canada is increasing, but increasing less rapidly than that of Japan, which, we remember, imports almost all of her iron ore. Second, the steel per capita figure for the United States is more than 50 per cent higher than that of Canada and the United Kingdom. And, bringing this back to the general topic in hand, we must emphasize the fact that American production is based upon ores of which some 20 per cent are shipped from Canada. Iron ore exports from Canada to the United States almost doubled between 1960 and 1963.

Our production of manufactured goods in Canada must increase, but the trend during the past ten years or so has not been very encouraging. Data published by the Organization for Economic Co-operation and Development show that the over-all rate of increase of output per capita in Canada is lower than that of any other industrialized country. Table IV shows that in our production of manufactured goods, we are barely keeping pace. Tables V and VI show production figures for two commodities whose manufacture squeezes every penny from the raw material. Canada's position is poor.

Canadian production of radio and television sets does not show any improvement over five years, while that of Japan has increased more than threefold, and that of the United States has increased by about 50 per cent. Canadian manufacture of cars shows an increase that parallels that of the United States. Perhaps we should expect this for our car production is really part of that of the United States. But we cannot overlook the fact that while the increase has resulted in an economic boon, production in Japan and the United Kingdom has increased more rapidly than has ours.

It is at this point that we strike a hard truth: that while our industries that produce raw metal are to a considerable extent Canadian-owned, or if not Canadian-owned, they depend upon an integrated Canadian effort, our fabricating industries are much more predominantly American-owned and are substantially production lines located in Canada. Under these circumstances, I see little

TABLE IV*

Canadian exports as a share of world exports
(Per cent of current values)

	1954	1955	1956	1957	1958	1959	1960	1961	1962
Total Canadian exports	4.7	4.7	4.8	4.6	4.7	4.7	4.4	4.4	4.2
Canadian exports of primary products	n.a.	3.7	4.3	4.3	4.7	4.7	4.3	4.6	n.a.
Processed materials	n.a.	13.7	12.1	11.4	11.5	11.3	10.7	10.5	n.a.
Manufactured products (n.a.–not available)	n.a.	3.3	1.4	1.5	1.6	1.4	1.3	1.4	n.a.

*Data from United Nations and Organization for Economic Co-operation and Development, as taken from *Economic Goals for Canada to 1970* (Economic Council of Canada, 1964).

TABLE V

Radio and TV sets produced

		1000's of units			Units per 1,000 population, 1962
		1948	1958	1962	
Canada	TV	—	—	15	1
	Radio	640	745	660	36
United States	TV	975	5,281	6,644	36
	Radio	16,708	12,734	19,619	105
United Kingdom	TV	91	1,998	1,463	27
	Radio	1,630	1,808	2,977	56
Japan	TV	—	1,191	4,885	51
	Radio	807	5,028	15,487	163

Data from *Statistical Yearbook, 1963*, United Nations.

TABLE VI

Motor vehicles wholly or mainly from domestic parts

	1000's of units			Units per 1,000 population, 1962
	1948	1958	1962	
Canada	164	360	501	27
United States	5,286	5,134	8,173	44
United Kingdom	511	1,364	1,674	31
Japan	37	286	1,124	11

Data from *Statistical Yearbook, 1963*, United Nations.

opportunity for change in the existing circumstances. That is, we will continue to export raw materials to the States —for that is our bread and butter—and the potential of fabricating our raw materials will largely be realized to the extent that the United States wishes. This is not intended to be a complaint; I simply state the facts as I see them.

Indeed, it may be argued that such a relationship is to our benefit, for, being tied to an industrial giant, we have some assurance of industrial stability. But rather than try to argue on either side of the debate, I will present what seem to me to be two crucial aspects of the Canadian-American relationships that relate to use of raw materials.

The hope of sharing the earth's resources so that what has recently been referred to as "the banquet of life" can offer more than a few crumbs to the majority of the world, is more of a political problem than a technological one or, if I may say so, than a religious one. Or, at least, if it becomes a technological problem, it will be one of distribution—a matter of distributing people and commodities —which may well tax our ingenuity even more than our pocketbooks. Regrettably, however, we have not been put to this technological test and the white person born on the North American continent has many accidental advantages to which he is not particularly entitled.

I see no quick solution to the inequities that surround us. There is, in the jargon of the chemist, what is known as a "rate-controlling reaction" in any process. The rate-controlling step in our own civilizations appear to be that of social change; the technology is there, but the means of disseminating and assimilating technological change is restricted by ignorance and the lure of the quick buck.

In the absence of a panacea that would let us fulfil those obligations of equality, goodwill, and all the rest that we subscribe to when it is convenient to do so, the most obvious part-solution seems to me to be to open Canada much more widely to immigrants. There may be temporary difficulties in greater immigration. We need, specifically, trained men, and good technicians. And, while we think we need craftsmen and tradesmen, we cannot be so sure of this, because automation is already thundering upon us. Whatever the temporary problems, Canada should be able to support a great population for, not only can it grow food, but it has raw materials—minerals—for exploitation. These represent an intrinsic wealth that can be parlayed into a livelihood for many millions of people who, at present, are not able to fulfil their own potential.

There are many obstacles in the way of this hope. We must be prepared to take people who, for the first generation may suffer the hardships that press upon a man through a lack of education, and, we may have a depression. The point is, that while the United States is reasonably well populated, Canada is under-populated. If Canada is to increase her population effectively, then she will have to export more fabricated products and less raw material to the States.

Putting aside the humanitarian aspects of the case for a moment, and looking at the problem in cold business terms, we should realize that an increase in population is in any case necessary to our own Canadian economy. At present, the fabrication of products is restricted because our domestic market is too small. It is difficult to produce any commodity when it, and all the spare parts and services that go with it, is produced in ten times that amount only a few miles away on the same continent. Even enterprising Canadians have been unable to produce manufactured goods, unless they were protected by tariff, simply because they were unable to offer the same variety and services as the American plant. An enthusiastic industrialist in Windsor would have some difficulty in setting up a plant to manufacture typewriters, if an American manufacturer in Detroit has those resources that are associated with a domestic market geared to ten times the population.

Paradoxically it is those countries that have so few raw materials (Western Europe and Japan) which seem to be the most inventive and productive in manufactured goods. Their ability to manufacture rests, to some extent, upon their attitude towards research and development, which I will consider in the next section. Before doing so, there is another topic to deal with, which equally offers a link with the subject of research and development.

The automotive industry in Canada annually produces in excess of $1 billion worth of cars. The value of cars made in Canada is about one-half the dollar value of our total exports and it is roughly equal to the dollar value of all the steel we make. The production of cars in Canada is about two-thirds per capita of that in the United States. While this may appear to be reasonably generous, we should ask ourselves whether Canadian participation in the automotive industry is really representative of what goes into a car. The statistics show that a reasonable number of Canadians work towards the production of cars sold in Canada. But a closer examination shows that the production represents only one aspect of the industry —that of the production line. The engineering and the research and development that go into a car are almost entirely a United States enterprise. Again, this is not intended as a complaint, although the situation does alarm me. I am, however, simply drawing attention to a fact that is often forgotten; that is, American ownership or dominance, while it offers employment to Canadians, only offers it in restricted areas—predominantly labour. And the area which, for want of a better word I shall call "professional" is lean in the Canadian activities of American-owned companies. This is true not only of the automotive business, but in oil and gas, electronics, and chemicals.

This imbalance will have a degenerative effect upon our technology, economy, and education. The industry that is largely directed from outside the country and whose engineering and research are also performed abroad, does not make a substantial contribution to Canadian technological endeavour. The normal movement of engineers and research workers from one industry to another provides an over-all enrichment of the technology, but the automotive and other American-owned industries make little contribution to this sort of development, for their engineering and research are conducted in the United States. Further, American universities, and particularly their engineering faculties, derive strength from a proximity of engineering staff in industry. We, in Canada, do not have the proper proportion of such specialists in our industrial communities.

I am not sure that the automotive trade pact will help this situation so far as Canadians are concerned for, while a "Canadian content" is assured, the means of attaining that content are not spelled out. I rather fear that, unless Canadians are more astute in their planning than they have been in the past, they will find that while the pact may improve industrial production for the time being, the long-term effect will not encourage any obvious improvement in technological activities. Probably the only way of ensuring that all aspects of Canadian technical and professional skills are to be utilized in a Canadian-based automotive plant is to establish a Crown company to manufacture a Canadian car. The trade pact, while it improves our production lines, obviously does not fulfil the hopes of the Economic Council that we might improve our technology through Canadian research and development.

The comparatively small Canadian expenditure (as a percentage of GNP) on research and development has aroused pleas from the Economic Council which have been followed by some spirited rebuttals. Figures that compare our research expenditure with that in the United States are not very meaningful. Our major industries, in the context of this paper, are those that produce raw materials or metal, not manufactured goods. Hence research is directed principally to the production of metal. Research in this area is generally conducted in the plant.

In contrast, for example, to the electronics industry, where research demands extensive laboratory facilities, the primary metal producers are able to use their plant as laboratory. Hence their research expenditures involve only personnel, and, indeed, often the research is to some extent effected by those people who are simply on the job and may not be specifically hired as research engineers. It is natural, then, that our research expenditure based on GNP appears to be low. The figure simply tells us that we have few Canadian-owned manufacturing industries.

The subject of our industrial research effort is not a new one in Canada. We tend to forget that the National Research Council was formed in 1916 to report to and advise the federal government on Canada's scientific and industrial research. The result of NRC's work was the establishment of laboratories and the encouragement and financing of university and industrial research. The 1965 budget of NRC (about $68 million) represents roughly equal amounts for the operation of the Council's laboratories and for the support of outside research, mainly in universities.

The Scientific Secretariat, established in 1963, today has similar terms of reference to those that originally directed the National Research Council and the new Department of Industry has the personnel and funds to encourage industrial development. The Mines Branch of the Department of Mines and Technical Surveys has as its objective the development, at all stages of processing, of Canada's mineral reserves. Several provincial research councils fulfil the same kind of function, that of encouraging Canadian industrial development. Direct grants, tax incentive programs of such generosity that even the Treasury cannot understand them, and co-operation from federal and provincial sources add to the incentive for

Canadian manufacturers to research their processes, raw materials, and products.

It is too early to appraise the success of these incentives. It is not, however, too early to appreciate that direction and guidance are lacking. In what areas is industrial development most promising? In what subjects should we rely upon imported technology? In what products do we have a peculiarly Canadian advantage? To what extent should universities be expected and encouraged to contribute to a national effort?

Industrial research in Canada is patchy and defeats simple analysis, but a few generalizations can be made. First, Canadian companies that were formed by severance from American industry (some metal-making and chemical industries) are active in research and development. Second, Canadian-based companies originally concerned only with the sale of metal are now much more active in the development of products through research in Canada (the ferrous and non-ferrous metal industries). Third, American-owned manufacturing industries (notably the car producers) conduct all their research in the United States. Fourth, small manufacturing industries are generally not involved in research as they probably cannot afford the capital outlay, despite financial incentives.

I am most concerned about the third and fourth categories. The small industries that I mentioned cannot use financial incentives offered them by the government, since even under these conditions, they cannot afford to establish their own laboratories and staff. More surprisingly, they are often unaware of the assistance that can be given them by research organizations—federal, provincial, and private—which may be permitted to take projects that are subcontracted to them. The small industry in need of research and development should be encouraged to seek the help of well-equipped and well-staffed laboratories.

It is with this intention in mind that the Faculty of Applied Science at the University of Windsor plans to establish a research institute for the service of local industries that cannot justify or that wish to complement their own research facilities.

The category of American-owned companies that perform all their research in the United States leads to the same kind of imbalance in our society that I referred to in connection with their general engineering activities. However, I would not expect these companies to be particularly impressed by an argument that appealed only to a sense of social well-being. I wish, however, that they would more carefully analyse the case for conducting some of their research in Canada. The argument that company research of all kinds must be conducted at the same location is inept. Researchers all over the world work together; and often the worst communications exist between the engineers in adjacent laboratories. There are, in fact, many areas of engineering research that are particularly appropriate to Canada.

While the availability of federal research contracts is more restricted in Canada than in the United States, I suspect that the situation would improve were more Canadian manufacturing industries to make demands. The tax incentive arrangements offer a cheap research dollar; and the salaries of Canadian research engineers and scientists are rather less than those in the United States.

In the context of Canadian-American planning, I shall conclude by making the following suggestions:

That Canada's productivity of manufactured goods will only increase as our population expands. Export of manufactured goods relies upon a solid domestic market which Canada, in view of its proximity to the United States, lacks. Hence we should encourage immigrants.

Any sharp increase in our production of manufactured

goods depends upon the availability of capital. If Canadians follow their usual pattern, they will be reluctant to invest; hence the funds will be generated from foreign sources, and we shall provide ourselves with grist to our grievance mill.

As our production, and hence our export, of manufactured goods increases, so must our export of raw materials to the United States be curtailed. There is, after all, a limit to the courtesies one extends to one's competitors.

Guidance, even direction, in the matter of industrial research and development must be offered. But perhaps the complexity of this problem is reflected by the complex internal interactions of the government establishments that seek to solve it.

The most serious problem, and one that is most often ignored, is the degenerative effect of the lack of Canadian engineering and research enterprise in Canadian-based, American-owned manufacturing industries.

While I am reluctant to suggest government intervention in this matter, I have no other solution to offer than an exploration of the possibilities of legislation to ensure that American-owned companies in Canada conduct an amount of research in Canada that is equivalent with the American research effort. This is vital to the development of a technology competent and properly balanced society. Without it we simply become the peasantry in a North American industrial feudalism.

VII. THE HUMAN PRICE OF PLANNING

PAUL YLVISAKER*

THE TOPIC, "The Human Price of Planning," is a standard one that I will not deal with in a very standard way. The traditional way of handling it goes back to those ideological and political disputes of the 1920's and 1930's when we divided into conservative and liberal camps, and we worried and warred over the question of whether government should be allowed to intervene in the natural order of things. The human benefits of intervening were counted in welfare terms and the human cost was feared to be a loss of liberty. Philosophically, I think this question still may have some appeal. Politically, at least in the United States as recent elections have shown, the question is beginning to produce ennui.

The topic is the "human price of planning," rather than the "human cost," because in that subtle shift of phrasing, I can see how one can make this question relevant to the mysteries and mischief of our times. My underlying argument is going to be that in our day we plan, if we plan

*Director, Public Affairs Program, Ford Foundation, New York.

at all, by paying the price exacted by an extraordinarily diverse, sophisticated, and ever more powerful citizen public, in a political setting which is considerably different from, and far more complex than, that in which the Keynesians and Roosevelts wrenched themselves free from the dying hand of the past.

So far, most people find this price of planning, and the differences between our generations, in terms of simple numbers—we are X millions more, therefore the tax burden must be X billions greater. By sticking to these mere quantities we can extrapolate all the other requirements, without either stretching our minds or shrinking our prejudices. Thus, for a population increase of a factor of two, or five, or ten, we will have to have an equivalent increase in the same kinds of bureaucrats, the same university training-programs to produce them, guided by ten times more, the same kind of industrial advisers, economic consultants supporting research, legislative investigators, and governmental apparatus in connecting points between the citizen and his authority. I argue and fear that this drives us straight into the failures of planning that we are witnessing today.

Perhaps it is time to begin perceiving qualities rather than quantities, and to base our efforts to plan on essential changes in social characteristics and in public behaviour patterns—changes which have been taking place with lightning rapidity in the last thirty years.

In the 1930's planning was a relatively unknown and untested remedy which was argued over by an informed and/or prejudiced few in the name of the masses. When the battle was won, as by President Roosevelt, it was a battle won against the cold enemy, which was seen as an influential minority hostile to the general public. When planning was implemented, it was viewed largely as a national exercise by economic technicians using monetary and fiscal devices to achieve stable growth and full employment, both of which were measured in statistical aggregates. However, in the 1960's, the debate over planning has moved, I think properly, from the general to the specific. We live so immediately within the future that it seems ridiculous not to plan for it. But, while everybody these days seems to be willing to hire planners (and now they are working in every part and every level of our society), we have all become extremely resistant to the idea that anybody should tell us what to do. This is happening not only in the United States but also in other countries which I have visited, for example, the Soviet Union.

So behold the present irony. Since the 1930's the masses have adopted both ends of that political spectrum. They have adopted both the concept of planning and that of *laissez-faire*. *Laissez-faire* in our times is no longer the doctrine of the minority, it is the doctrine of the majority of extremely recalcitrant and unpredictable citizens who do not want anybody to tell them what to do. To see this irony at work, you have only to attend the meetings of your local planning and zoning boards. Everybody there will agree that we ought to have orderly growth in development of our communities. But, from that point on, there is little agreement, particularly when the question comes down to whether, for example, apartments should be allowed in single family neighbourhoods, or whether one-acre zoning is the proper way to achieve orderly growth, or whether you are going to have the sewage system in your community. Or follow through the efforts these days to beautify our highways, reduce traffic congestion, stop air pollution, or clean up our rivers and streams. We support the planners all the way, until they tell us to take down our highway sign, to park our car inside, to stop burning our trash, and to raise our taxes to build that new sewage-treatment plant. This public ambivalence—the acceptance of planning and the hostility to it—is one of those changing conditions that the new art of planning has to take into account. Let me mention a few of the other changes, as I see them, that have taken place since the 1930's:

1. Certainly the need for planning has now suffused itself through every level of our society, especially the problems of planning our cities. I would argue that the problem of planning our cities is probably as important an issue, or very close to it, as planning for the national defense and full employment. Nor can it be separated from these two. The cities are the new frontier of planning, and I would advise those who are dealing in an older way with economic planning at a national level that the competition is going to be extremely severe.

2. The scope of planning is no longer limited to the economic sector. In the United States, we have seen recently the emergence of social planning in the poverty program under Sargent Shriver. I have recently been in conversation with the Minister of Housing and Local Government in Britain and know that, despite the immigration quotas that are being applied in order to restrict entry, in London, the Midlands, and elsewhere, they are soon coming to social planning at the local level in a way which will again contend, along with efforts at the national level, to keep full employment.

3. The goals of planning can no longer be limited to statements of aggregates. The Negro, the aged, and the young, have taught us that we cannot use aggregates. There may be 4 or 5 per cent unemployment in the aggregate, but 15, 20, or 25 per cent unemployment in certain age groups: the aged who have become poor one year after turning 65; or the young who are unemployed in too many instances. Also you can have national aggregates of

affluence while in depressed regions the problems of economic and social planning are great.

4. That lingering tendency to have two planning games —one national and economic, the other local, physical, and social; the one presided over by the economists, the other largely by the fiscal planner and now, in the U.S., the social planner—can no longer be indulged in. Different schools of thought represent the kind of aggregate economist who said that it is a problem of expanding the whole pie and therefore we ought to continue to work as we have, and others who recognize that you also had to work at structural unemployment, or the frictions, the inefficiencies, and the special problems of certain groups. The two were resolved in a patch-up way, in the United States, by having one local social planning program and then continuing the national economies. But this tendency to separate cannot long survive.

5. Planning is no longer an exercise for a few technocrats or for a few political champions. It is now a necessity for the masses.

6. The public is now well versed in the mysteries of the art of planning and in its failures. This is different from the 1930's, where it was still a bit of mystic and magic and it was argued in the abstract. But we have had thirty years of it now: its successes have been considerable and its failures have been tragic and many. The public, at least as I have seen it in Japan, in India and the Soviet Union, as well as in the U.S., is becoming experienced, wise, sceptical, versed in the art of opposing and exposing, and ready to veto. There are many examples where a public first touched by planning in a reform sense has reacted with a kind of scepticism. Urban renewal has become known in many cases as Negro removal. A green belt is more and more often being defined as that belt which separates a white belt from a black belt. We have had

zoning for orderly development, which excludes people that are not wanted—for example, a point system in a nearby community went into the social background of a group before they could move into that community. These kinds of planning, which have been used with one stated purpose and another in practice, are leading to a sceptical and aroused public. This public now wants to be planned with and not for.

7. The old ignorances and fears which are reciprocals of the last point, can no longer be relied upon to ensure compliance. More and more, in sophisticated society, we are going to be moving from regulations and controls to incentives.

8. A national competence to act, without local equivalents, has become an exercise in frustration. It is interesting to watch at our national level, when a national problem is defined and a program adopted, how many times it fails because there is not a local competence to work with it. The employment service in the U.S. is great in its national conception and very poor in its local administration. Emerging is a group of mayors who appreciate this problem. Very shortly I think you will see developing the kind of administration which has councils of economic advisers, and State of the City, as well as State of the Union, messages. But, this in turn is going to lead to reciprocal power, which means that a mayor must be bargained with by the President of the United States before planning at either level can succeed.

9. The old syndrome that for every public purpose there is a public agency has come into question. In our society, the public purpose can be accomplished through a variety of agencies, and not necessarily public ones. More and more the political executive, who is sensitive to the consumers' needs, is struggling against his own bureaucracy to effect the programs he wants to carry out. I call this the crisis of modern bureaucracy.

10. The old lines of distinction between public and private are fading and people are willing to admit that planning does not necessarily lead to control. But, ultimately it is the individual who is affected by planning—the individual who will ask, "Does it work?" "Will it help?" and "What has it meant?" Until the government and society recognize the individual in the context of planning the answers to these questions will not be favourable and the price of human planning will be high.

Some implications for planners emerge from these considerations:

First, they must recognize that planning is an untidy art—call it a political art or the art of social bargaining, if you will. No longer in this complicated society, which each man holding a share of power, can you expect technocrats with tidy assumptions to begin to plan effectively. Around the planning table are the adversaries who, in our democratic structure, are used to the idea of bargaining for a solution.

It is interesting to note here that when we asked people to evaluate the poverty program and some of the social planing programs in which the Ford Foundation has been involved—in Detroit, Oakland and elsewhere—the answers have been varied. Men who came to qualify or to use existing tidy methods or disciplines have failed. Those who succeeded have captured the intangibles.

Second, planning will have to be a listening art. Planners will often have to listen to those who are outside their jurisdiction, outside their social clubs, and to those things which may not appear important, at a time when they are not ready for them. For example, we did not normally listen to the students of the University of California at Berkeley. But these students, as well as some in North Carolina and community members in other parts of the United States, have begun shaking the structure, not merely of the university, but that of the community of which they are a part. We had assumed that we did not listen to a student until he could vote, but we are learning quite differently.

In the United States there are Negroes and others living in deep poverty. Even if the Negro population is only 10–11 per cent of the total, there is abroad the statement of equality to which we all subscribe. A minority with a just cause can shake a majority with a bad conscience. Planning thus involves the art of listening to people to whom you normally do not listen to, when you do not want to, or when it is not convenient to do so.

Third, I have argued that planning is the art of sharing. Certainly in our system of democracy, where power is a reciprocal function, participation in planning may be far more important than the technical results when participation is not encouraged. Already a sophisticated judgment is growing out of the American poverty program. For all the mistakes made in Harlem, for all the administrative bungling, for even those times when the public purse is not adequately accounted for, the fact that the Negroes have been allowed and encouraged to take part in improving their situation is far more important than the results of a technical exercise.

Fourth, the basic assumptions of the technicians and politicians who take up planning as an art must be challenged. For example, the planning of education in the United States is usually a quantitative proposition—we have so many children, therefore we need so many more universities, and so many more teachers, etc. A young British anthropologist challenged this assumption when he said, "In your society those children who have the best capacities to take on life early are those who are longest kept in the educational hot-house. Those children who have the least capacity, the least maturity, the least advantage and stability are thrown or allowed to drop out at fourteen and fifteen, and no structural provision is made for them. . . ." Planners will plan, in many cases to expand their programs, using the wrong tools.

Planning in our society will have to be linked with competition in the public sector. It is strange that the democratic, capitalistic orders that we have known have insisted on free enterprise in the private sector and allowed a monopoly to grow in the public sector. The government enforces competition in the private sector through the Sherman and Interstate Commerce Acts and later antitrust legislation, but there is little to ensure competition in the public sector. What is emerging in most of our societies, the sociologists point out, is the growth of a non-profit sector. We may now get a declaration of public purpose, but there are alternate ways of accomplishing it—through federal, state, or local governments; through industry on contract; through private associations; or, as in the United States poverty program, the deliberate creation of non-profit private sector organizations to accomplish a public purpose. This may be a breakthrough against what I called "the crisis of bureaucracy." A bureaucratic organization may now build up parallel organization—private, non-private, or semi-private—to counteract stagnation from within.

Planning may also be linked with its apparent opposite. Local counterparts to the national administration are needed, and it may well be that the art of planning will include the encouragement of decentralized forms of action in a pluralistic society.

Finally, the art of planning must be considered in terms of accomplishments. The public demands of the planners, "Do not play games with us!" The Watts area of Los Angeles is a good example of a community that has been worked over by planners at every level from the national economic planners, who talk about total employment, to the local social planners, who are running the poverty program. The Negroes are now completely resistant to anybody who goes through the gestures of planning and does not produce results. This is a healthy attitude, which not only the Negroes of Watts but the under-privileged everywhere have been expressing in the United States for the last three or four years.

The final judgment of the art of the planners comes from the people who ask of them, "What is the product?" "Have you merely played games?" and "What happens at the other end?" This is the human price of planning.

Now looking forward, as I consign this art of planning to the politician or to the technocrat, I do not envy him, but I do have a kind of feeling of rejoicing for the liberated public.

EPILOGUE

WE HAVE DISCUSSED planning in the context of different areas of Canadian-American affairs—business, labour, resources development, and research efforts. Although there were contrasting interpretations of what planning is, the range of papers filled in the outline of planning drawn up by Dr. Johnson who described planning in the Canadian-American context as "the general process of attempting to take stock of the present situation and its evolving trends, predict the general direction of future developments, assess these in the light of generally accepted social and economic goals, and where necessary formulate programs and policies designed to shape future developments as closely as possible to conform to what is considered to be in the social interest." Many of the subsequent papers on planning—official and business—echoed this approach, stressing the need for vision based on discernment of where we are and where we are going.

Dr. Ylvisaker added a very cogent warning that this future focus, however skilfully related to what we now know, may not be enough. Pointing to recent events at Berkeley and Watts in California, he cautioned us also to keep our eyes and ears open to the immediate and unexpected—to listen, as he said, "to those who are often not normally listened to." Specifically, he said, we should listen to those not in "our club"—to those we may not think important, and we should do this even when we are not ready to act. Dr. Ylvisaker gave us, therefore, a second focus for planning. We should, he seems to suggest, supplement our concern for resolving issues as they are now perceived in a way benefiting our children's children, by concern for the unanticipated questions behind today's headlines. In other words, those involved in Canadian-American planning have a second reason for being modest: they must not think they know all the problems.

In the Introduction Dr. Johnson identified several promising areas for Canadian-American joint planning: the liberalization of trade, the use of energy, the use of water resources, and the organization of transportation. Of these, the first three were discussed. Transportation, perhaps surprisingly, was not covered at all. But in its place Mr. Cisler opened the vista of a new and perhaps urgent area for common efforts: that of urban planning. The Doxiadis study, which Mr. Cisler discussed, foresees by the end of the century a new "megalopolis," similar to the almost continual city between Boston and Washington, stretching from Milwaukee and Chicago to Toronto and Buffalo. This area is expected to become a flood plain for an expanding population and a locus for all the problems which we now recognize the modern urban environment incubates.

Indeed, the problem of planning today's cities has been called our most pressing frontier area. Dr. Ylvisaker suggested it "has become hardly less important than planning for national defence and full employment." Into it we are directing vast resources of brainpower and money in an attempt to effect breakthroughs in programs for urban renewal and rapid transit, and at a more basic level, in attempts to come to grips with the real causes of urban poverty.

The emergence of a Chicago-Toronto megalopolis raises the prospect of this frontier area of urban challenges developing on both sides of the Canadian-American border. And it raises the question of whether in the coming years the most vital area for joint planning may not be in this growing common urban region, rather than in trade, energy, water, or transportation. The nature of such planning would of course involve, as does the Doxiadis study, looking ahead to what we can anticipate on the basis of present facts and trends. But we should also follow Dr. Ylvisaker's advice and be prepared to listen together for unexpected stirrings in unexpected places and be able to fashion sudden unprecedented responses to sudden unprecedented challenges.

Lightning Source UK Ltd.
Milton Keynes UK
UKHW012358200722
406167UK00001B/320